TO ACCESS YOUR ONLINE VIDEOS EMAIL YOUR RECEIPT TO:

jullien@careerchangechallenge.com

AND YOU WILL RECEIVE A USERNAME AND PASSWORD WITH 24 HOURS.

CAREER CHANGE CHALLENGE

Proven Secrets & Strategies To Get Your D.R.E.A.M. Job In 30 Days Or Less

MVMT
ATTN: Department of Motivated Vehicles
155 Water Street
Brooklyn, NY 11201

Copyright © 2010 Jullien Gordon

All rights reserved, including the right to reproduce this book or portions thereof in any form whatsoever. For more information address The Department of Motivated Vehicles, 155 Water Street, Brooklyn, NY 11201.

For more information about speaking engagements or special discounts for bulk purchase, please contact The Department of Motivated Vehicles at (646) 875-8477 or info@motivatedvehicles.com.

Manufactured in the United States of America

CAREER

1. A sequence of professional opportunities (jobs, projects, freelance, internships, education) doing work one cares deeply about for and/or with other people (company, customer, constituents).

2. Speed.

CHANGE

1. An intentional process of moving something from some point A to some point B.

2. An involuntary process constantly working for our greatest good and growth.

CHALLENGE

1. An event that requires effort beyond one's average output.

2. A bet on one's self to achieve something they and/or others doubted was possible.

3. To push someone to and/or beyond their perceived limits.

1. Create Your D.R.E.A.M. Life
Career & Life Visioning & Financial Planning

1.1 HOW TO DREAM AGAIN
1.2 HOW TO ENROLL YOUR FRIENDS IN YOUR CAREER CHANGE PROCESS

FINANCIAL FREEDOM
1.3 HOW TO CALCULATE YOUR FINANCIAL FREEDOM
1.4 HOW TO BUDGET FOR YOUR CAREER CHANGE
1.5 HOW TO CALCULATE YOUR CURRENT & DESIRED PROFESSIONAL VELOCITY
1.6 HOW TO OVERCOME OTHER BARRIERS TO EXIT

INNER-VIEWING
1.7 HOW TO CREATE YOUR PERSONAL SUCCESS DASHBOARD
1.8 HOW TO IDENTIFY YOUR PASSIONS
1.9 HOW TO IDENTIFY A PROBLEM THAT MATTERS TO YOU
1.10 HOW TO IDENTIFY YOUR TARGET MARKET
1.11 HOW TO FIND YOUR NICHE & POSITION YOURSELF TO WIN
1.12 HOW TO THINK LIKE A CAREER PIONEER
1.13 HOW TO CREATE YOUR CAREER VISION
1.14 HOW TO LEAVE A LEGACY
1.15 HOW TO CREATE YOUR 30 SECOND PITCH

CURRENT JOB ASSESSMENT
1.16 HOW TO MEASURE YOUR ALIGNMENT WITH YOUR EXISTING COMPANY
1.17 HOW TO EVALUATE WHAT ACTIVITIES FULFILL YOU AND DEPLETE YOU
1.18 HOW TO MAKE SURE YOU DON'T REPEAT THE SAME MISTAKE TWICE

SKILLS & STRENGTHS DEVELOPMENT
1.19 HOW TO ASSESS YOUR CURRENT SKILL SET
1.20 HOW TO SEND YOUR 30 DAY DO IT RECAP EMAIL
1.21 HOW TO IDENTIFY YOUR TOP 5 STRENGTHS

2. Attract Your D.R.E.A.M. Career
Personal Branding Online & Offline, Resume, & Cover Letter

2.1 HOW TO GET YOUR FRIENDS' INSIGHTS ON YOUR PERSONAL BRAND

PACKAGING
2.2 HOW TO GET TESTIMONIALS FROM PEOPLE WHO KNOW YOU
2.3 HOW TO CREATE PROFESSIONAL BUSINESS CARDS FOR CHEAP
2.4 HOW TO CREATE PROFESSIONAL HEAD SHOTS AT HOME
2.5 HOW TO WRITE THE WORLD'S BEST RESUME EVER
2.6 HOW TO THINK, TALK, & ACT LIKE YOU ALREADY WORK THERE
2.7 HOW TO WRITE A GREAT COVER LETTER
2.8 HOW TO SET YOURSELF APART WITH A RESUME 2.0 OR PORTFOLIO

WEBSITE & BLOG
2.9 HOW TO CREATE A FREE WEBSITE THAT WOOS POTENTIAL EMPLOYERS
2.10 HOW TO BUY WWW.YOURNAME.COM AND GET FIRSTNAME@YOURNAME.COM
2.11 HOW TO USE 3 SIMPLE & SHORT BLOGS TO SHOW YOU ARE COMPETENT
2.12 HOW TO EDIT ALL OF YOUR COPY FOR CONSISTENCY & GRAMMAR

SOCIAL NETWORKING
2.13 HOW TO MAXIMIZE YOUR LINKEDIN PROFILE & EXPAND YOUR NETWORKS
2.14 HOW TO MAXIMIZE YOUR FACEBOOK PROFILE & EXPAND YOUR NETWORKS

3. Build Your D.R.E.A.M. Team

Networking Up, Down, & Across, Relationship Management, & Follow Up

NETWORKING PREPARATION
3.1 HOW TO BUILD YOUR SOCIAL CAPITAL IN 30 DAYS
3.2 HOW TO LEAVE WITH REAL RELATIONSHIPS, NOT JUST BUSINESS CARDS
3.3 HOW TO SHARPEN YOUR 30 SECOND PITCH DELIVERY
3.4 HOW TO SOUND LIKE AN EXPERT AT ANY NETWORKING EVENT
3.5 HOW TO FIND GREAT NETWORKING EVENTS

FOLLOWING UP
3.6 HOW TO FOLLOW UP USING T.E.C.H.
3.7 HOW TO EXECUTE A POWERFUL 30-MINUTE GET LINKED IN CONVERSATION

MENTORSHIP
3.8 HOW TO NETWORK UP & FIND MENTORS
3.9 HOW TO ASK AND ENGAGE MENTORS

4. Land Your D.R.E.A.M. Job
Job Search Online & Offline, Interviewing, & Negotiation

MAXIMIZING WHERE YOU ARE
4.1 HOW TO LEAVE THE DOOR OPEN AT YOUR OLD JOB
4.2 HOW TO USE THE TIME YOU STILL HAVE AT YOUR OLD JOB TO GET YOUR NEW JOB

JOB SEARCH
4.3 HOW TO USE GOOGLE & OTHER JOB SEARCH ENGINES TO SEARCH FOR JOBS FASTER
4.4 HOW TO CREATE YOUR VERY OWN JOB "PERCH" ENGINE
4.5 HOW TO USE FACEBOOK, LINKEDIN, & TWITTER TO FIND JOBS

INNER-VIEWING & INTER-VIEW PREP
4.6 HOW TO PROPERLY RESEARCH A CAREER PATH FOR FIT-NESS
4.7 HOW TO PROPERLY RESEARCH A COMPANY SO YOU INTERVIEW AS FEW TIMES AS POSSIBLE
4.8 HOW TO IDENTIFY THE PROBLEM THEY ARE HIRING YOU TO SOLVE
4.9 HOW TO REPURPOSE, REPOSITION, & TRANSFER EVERYTHING YOU'RE DOING NOW TO HELP YOU STAND OUT

INTER-VIEWING & OVER-VIEWING
4.10 HOW TO ANSWER THE TOP 20 INTERVIEW QUESTIONS WITH CONFIDENCE
4.11 HOW TO KEEP A POTENTIAL EMPLOYER ENGAGED AFTER THE INTERVIEW

NEGOTIATION
4.12 HOW TO DETERMINE YOUR VALUE & WHAT YOU'RE WORTH

FIRST 3 MONTHS
4.13 HOW TO CREATE A POWERFUL 3 YEAR PLAN & PREPARE FOR YOUR NEXT CAREER MOVE NOW
4.14 HOW TO HAVE AN AMAZING FIRST 3 MONTHS

30 DAY CAREER CHANGE CHALLENGE CALENDAR

WK	MON	TUES	WED	THUR	FRI	SAT	SUN
1	1.1 ___ 1.2 1.3 V:28 min A:60 min	1.4 ___ 1.5 1.6 V:16 min A:80 min	1.7 ___ 1.8 V:16 min A:90 min	1.9 ___ 1.10 1.11 V:17 min A:95 min	1.12 ___ 1.13 V:17 min A:70 min	1.14 ___ 1.15 1.16 V:18 min A:80 min	1.17 ___ 1.18 V:10 min A:80 min
2	1.19 ___ 1.20 1.21 2.1 V:18 min A:75 min	2.2 ___ 2.3 2.4 V:15 min A:100 m.	2.5 V:40 min A:170 m.	2.6 ___ 2.7 V:10 min A:90 min	2.8 V:10 min A:90 min	2.9 V:13 min A:30 m.	2.10 V:34 min A:120 m.
3	2.11 ___ 2.12 V:10 min A:85 min	2.13 ___ 2.14 V:16 min A:50 min	3.1 V:6 min A:90 min	3.2 3.3 V:11 min A:75 min	3.4 3.5 3.6 V:16 min A:55 min	3.7 ___ 3.8 V:9 min A:75 min	3.9 V:9 min A:60 min
4	4.1 V:6 min A:60 min	4.2 ___ 4.3 V:15 min A:75 min	4.4 ___ 4.5 V:14 min A:55 min	4.6 ___ 4.7 V:8 min A:65 min	4.8 ___ 4.9 V:8 min A:80 min	4.10 ___ 4.11 V:21 min A:80 min	4.12 ___ 4.13 V:12 min A:80 min
5	4.14 ___ V:7 min A:60 min	FINISH MISSED WORK					

www.CareerChangeChallenge.com   Copyright © 2010 Jullien Gordon

30 DAY CAREER CHANGE CHALLENGE CHECKLIST

M1	VID	ACT	M2	VID	ACT	M3	VID	ACT	M4	VID	ACT
1			1			1			1		
2			2			2			2		
3			3			3			3		
4			4			4			4		
5			5			5			5		
6			6			6			6		
7			7			7			7		
8			8			8			8		
9			9			9			9		
10			10						10		
11			11						11		
12			12						12		
13			13						13		
14			14								
15											
16											
17											
18											
19											
20											
21											

www.CareerChangeChallenge.com

Copyright © 2010 Jullien Gordon

DELIVERABLES

[] Resume 1.0
[] Cover Letter
[] Website & Blog
[] Business Card
[] Resume 2.0 (Portfolio)
[] Updated LinkedIn Profile
[] Updated Facebook Profile
[] A copy of 10 business cards from people in your industry from networking
[] Off-boarding Presentation
[] Eulogy or 80 Year Old Toast
[] Retirement Speech
[] 3 Interview Confirmation Emails
[] Answers to Top 20 Interview Questions

CAREER CHANGE TO DO LIST

[]...

[]...

[]...

[]...

[]...

[]...

[]...

[]...

[]...

[]...

[]...

CAREER EXPLORATION SHEET

NEW PEOPLE TO EXPLORE

[]... []...

[]... []...

[]... []...

NEW INDUSTRIES TO EXPLORE

[]... []...

[]... []...

[]... []...

NEW CAREER PATHS TO EXPLORE

[]... []...

[]... []...

[]... []...

NEW SKILLS TO EXPLORE

[]... []...

[]... []...

[]... []...

NEW NEWS TO EXPLORE

[]... []...

[]... []...

NEW PROBLEMS/OPPORTUNITIES TO EXPLORE

[].. []..

[].. []..

[].. []..

NEW COMPANIES TO EXPLORE

[].. []..

[].. []..

[].. []..

NEW WEBSITES TO EXPLORE

[].. []..

[].. []..

[].. []..

NEW BOOKS TO EXPLORE

[].. []..

[].. []..

[].. []..

NEW TRENDS TO EXPLORE

[].. []..

[].. []..

NEW VOCABULARY WORDS TO EXPLORE

[] .... [] ....

[] .... [] ....

[] .... [] ....

NEW EVENTS/VENUES WORDS TO EXPLORE

[] .... [] ....

[] .... [] ....

[] .... [] ....

OTHER THINGS TO EXPLORE

[] .... [] ....

[] .... [] ....

[] .... [] ....

[] .... [] ....

[] .... [] ....

[] .... [] ....

[] .... [] ....

[] .... [] ....

[] .... [] ....

NEW CHOICES I'M MAKING REGARDING MY CAREER

....

....

....

....

....

....

THINGS I'M STILL INDECISIVE ABOUT BUT COMMIT TO RESEARCHING

....

....

....

....

....

....

ASSUMPTIONS I HAD, BUT WANT TO CHALLENGE ABOUT MY CAREER

....

....

....

....

....

....

MODULE ONE

Create Your D.R.E.A.M. Life

DAY 01

1.1 HOW TO DREAM AGAIN

Video Time: 13 minutes
Activity Time: 17 minutes

Required Tools:
- a D.R.E.A.M.

Language:
D.R.E.A.M. = Desired Relationships, Employment, & Money

Directions:
1. Dream about what your perfect average day would look like and write it down.
2. Dream about how you want your relationships to be and write it down.
3. Dream about how you want you your employment to be and write it down.
4. Dream about how you want your money to be and write it down.

I HAVE A DREAM & MY PERFECT AVERAGE DAY WOULD LOOK LIKE THIS:

06:00AM..

07:00AM..

08:00AM..

09:00AM..

10:00AM..

11:00AM..

12:00PM..

01:00PM..

02:00PM..

03:00PM..

04:00PM..

05:00PM..

06:00PM..

OTHER NOTES

....

....

....

....

....

PERFECT AVERAGE DAY CONTINUED...

07:00PM ....

08:00PM ....

09:00PM ....

10:00PM ....

11:00PM ....

12:00AM ....

01:00AM ....

02:00AM ....

03:00AM ....

04:00AM ....

05:00AM ....

06:00AM ....

OTHER NOTES

....

....

....

....

....

RELATIONSHIPS

My spouse and I..

....

....

My kids and I...

....

....

My parent/s and I...

....

....

My friends and I...

....

....

My colleagues and I..

....

....

My siblings and I..

....

....

My _____ **and I**..

....

EMPLOYMENT

In my eyes, the purpose of work is ....

....

I want to evaluate my career every .... **years**

I want to work in [] for-profit [] non-profit [] government [] a combination

I want to work for/with a [] big company [] small company [] startup [] myself

I want to work a maximum of [] 40 hr/week [] 60 hr/week [] 80+ hr/week

I want to work for/with a company that ....

....

....

I want to be in a work environment that ....

....

....

I want to work in a position that ....

....

....

I want to work with colleagues that ....

....

....

I expect my work & employer to ....

....

MONEY

INCOME
My mom made:........................ per year. My dad made:......................... per year.

I would be [] dissatisfied [] comfortable [] happy [] very happy with this much

Enough income would be $.....................Too much would be $............................

I want to give ....% of my income to good causes (ie church, charities, etc)

I intend to create $ .... in passive income annually by......................

....

SAVINGS
I want to save ....% of my income

I want to retire by the age of:......................with a savings of...............................

I intent to pay.....................% of my kids college loans

I will buy a house when I've saved....................... and/or have ....income

I will buy a car when I've saved......................... and/or have ....income

EXPENSES
The features of the house I want include:..

....

I want to buy my first house by the age of:..

The kind/s of car I want include:..

Some of the luxury items I want include:...

....

I want to go on .... personal vacations & .... family vacations every 4 years

Other major lifestyle expenses include:...

www.CareerChangeChallenge.com   Copyright © 2010 Jullien Gordon

1.2 HOW TO ENROLL YOUR FRIENDS IN YOUR CAREER CHANGE PROCESS

Video Time: 5 minutes
Activity Time: 15 minutes

Required Tools:
- 30 Day Do It Group Starter Kit

Language:
The 30 Day Do It = a fun group-based goal setting system that taps into positive peer pressure by encouraging friends to bet on their goals together

Directions:
1. Download the 30 Day Do It Group Starter Kit at http://ecourse.careerchangechallenge.com/wp-content/uploads/2010/08/30-Day-Do-It-Group-Starter-Kit.pdf.
2. List 16 people you would consider inviting based on the roles outlined in Vital Friends.
3. Email the invitation or use www.Evite.com to send an invitation.

START YOUR 30 DAY DO IT GROUP

Deciding Who To Invite

In the book *Vital Friends,* Tom Rath identifies 8 types of people you cannot afford to live without. List the first two names that come to mind for each type.

Type	Person #1	Person #2
1. Builder		
2. Collaborators		
3. Connectors		
4. Mind Openers		
5. Champions		
6. Companions		
7. Energizers		
8. Navigators		

Email Template

Edit and send the invitation below to all 16 people above with the expectation that only 6-10 will come. You can either send it as is using your regular email account, or try a service such as Evite.com, Pingg.com, and Facebook Events. And don't forget to invite me at jullien@goodexcusegoals.com.

SUBJECT: Career Goal Setting Party At My House, Wed. 7-8:30pm

BODY: Hello Friends,

I have a renewed commitment to advancing my career. Ultimately I'll either accelerate where I am or change. I want to invite you to join myself and others on this journey by having you come to a career goal setting party at my house at 1000 Monument Way, Brooklyn, NY 11243 on Wednesday night from 7-8:30pm. There will be people from a variety of industries also committed to professional development like you.

We're going to start at 7pm sharp. Bring your career goals or any other goal written down. I will provide the goal setting materials and some appetizers, but feel free to bring something if you would like. Please RSVP so that I can get a head count.

Cheers!

1.3 HOW TO CALCULATE YOUR FINANCIAL FREEDOM

Video Time: 10 minutes
Activity Time: 15 minutes

Required Tools:
- calculator
- monthly bills
- bank statements

Language:
Financial Capital = Who knows that you know what you know
Runway = The amount of time you can cover your basic monthly expenses if you chose to stop working today or got fired.

Statistics:
Forty-four percent of employees say they could go up to a month after losing their job before experiencing significant financial hardship, and another 27% say they could last up to four months. (http://www.gallup.com/poll/127511/One-Five-Americans-Fear-Job-Loss-Next-Months.aspx)

Directions:
1. Calculate and complete all of the yellow boxes.
2. Calculate your runway by dividing Total Assets by Total Monthly Expenses.

CURRENT MONTHLY EXPENSES

Line Item	Monthly Cost	Examples
Rent/Mortgage	$700	
Utilities	$100	gas, water, power
Phones	$200	home, cells
House Stuff	$50	internet, TV, supplies
Insurance	$60	health, home, etc
Entertainment	$150	movies, shows, etc
Food	$300	groceries, dining, etc
Automobile	$89	note, gas, insurance, tolls
Loans & Credit Cards	$810	student loans, etc
Other #1:		
Other #2:		**Minimum Annual Salary**
Total Monthly Expenses	$2459	$29508

CURRENT ASSETS

Source	Amount
Checking Account	$5400
Savings Account	$9000
Other #1:	
Other #2:	
Total Assets	$14400

Divide **Total Assets** by **Total Monthly Expense**.

If I quit my job or got laid off today, I would have a

5.8 month runway.

In order to save or invest half of my income each month, I need to earn 2 times my current monthly expenses which is

= $ **4,918** per month

x 12 months

= $ **59,016** per year

Considering, that the <u>profit margin in my industry</u> in my new industry is

= **25** %

I need to prove to my future employer that I can create at least

$ **59,016** / (100% - **25**%) = $ **59,016** / **0.75** =

= $ **78,688** in value (ie Revenue) per year or else it doesn't make sense for them to hire me.

	Industry	Profit Margin
1	Beverages - Brewers	25.9%
2	Closed-End Fund - Debt	25.3
3	REIT - Healthcare Facilities	24.6
4	Application Software	22.7
5	Information & Delivery Services	17.8
6	Cigarettes	17.4
7	Drug Manufacturers - Major	16.5
8	Networking & Communication Device	16.3
9	Agricultural Chemicals	15.2
10	Industrial Metals & Minerals	14.8
11	REIT - Residential	13.8
12	Security Software & Services	13.5
13	REIT - Retail	13.5
14	Drug Delivery	13.5
15	Railroads	12.9
16	Gas Utilities	12.6
17	Personal Products	12.3
18	Beverages - Wineries & Distillers	11.8
19	Education & Training Services	11.7
20	Diversified Communication Services	11.7
21	Wireless Communications	11.1
22	Personal Services	10
23	Oil & Gas Drilling & Exploration	9.7
24	Healthcare Information Services	9.3
25	Air Services, Other	9.2
26	Processed & Packaged Goods	9
27	Telecom Services - Domestic	8.9
28	Diversified Computer Systems	8.9
29	Diversified Utilities	8.8
30	Home Health Care	8.4
31	Oil & Gas Equipment & Services	8.3
32	Medical Laboratories & Research	8.2
33	Business Software & Services	8
34	Restaurants	7.5
35	Personal Computers	7.5
36	Food - Major Diversified	7.4
37	Foreign Regional Banks	7.3
38	Publishing - Books	7.1
39	Cleaning Products	7.1
40	Regional - Northeast Banks	7
41	Medical Instruments & Supplies	6.8
42	General Entertainment	6.8
43	Conglomerates	6.7
44	Biotechnology	6.7
45	Drugs - Generic	6.6
46	Textile - Apparel Footwear	6.4
47	Internet Information Providers	6.2
48	Telecom Services - Foreign	6.1
49	Electric Utilities	6.1
50	Sporting Activities	6
51	Research Services	5.8
52	Pollution & Treatment Controls	5.8
53	Auto Parts Stores	5.8
54	Beverages - Soft Drinks	5.7
55	Waste Management	5.6
56	Business Services	5.5
57	Small Tools & Accessories	5.3
58	Regional - Southwest Banks	5.3
59	Publishing - Periodicals	5.2
60	Aerospace Products & Services	5.2
61	Processing Systems & Products	5
62	Tobacco Products, Other	4.8
63	Metal Fabrication	4.8
64	Management Services	4.8
65	Recreational Vehicles	4.7
66	Aerospace Major Diversified	4.7
67	Oil & Gas Pipelines	4.6
68	Recreational Goods, Other	4.4
69	Information Technology Services	4.3
70	Consumer Services	4.3
71	Specialty Eateries	4.1
72	Auto Parts Wholesale	4
73	Accident & Health Insurance	3.8
74	Nonmetallic Mineral Mining	3.6
75	Insurance Brokers	3.6
76	Industrial Equipment & Components	3.6
77	**Hospitals**	**3.6**
78	Electronics Stores	3.6
79	Oil & Gas Refining & Marketing	3.5
80	Major Integrated Oil & Gas	3.5
81	Industrial Electrical Equipment	3.5
82	Data Storage Devices	3.5
83	Confectioners	3.5
84	Home Furnishing Stores	3.3
85	Heavy Construction	3.3
86	**Health Care Plans**	**3.3**

DAY 02

1.4 HOW TO BUDGET FOR YOUR CAREER CHANGE

Video Time: 5 minutes
Activity Time: 25 minutes

Required Tools:
- calculator

Language:
Bridge Job = a interim career opportunity someone takes to get from point A to point B on their career path. The opportunity is pre-determined to end within 18 months or when the career changer saves up a least a 6 month runway.

Directions:
1. Establish a budget for your career change.
2. Based on that budget, determine what combination of items you're willing to invest in. Your total budget should be equal or less than your pre-established budget.

CAREER CHANGE BUDGET

Since changing my career would be priceless, I am willing to set aside a budget of $_____ for my career change.

BASIC BUDGET

Line Item	Cost/Each	# of Each	Total Cost
Coffees	$10	10	$100
Lunches	$30	3	$90
Dinners	$50	2	$100
Thank You Cards	$20	1	$20
Padfolio	$25	1	$25
Business Cards	$20	1	$20
Domain Name	$10	1	$10
Books to Buy	$20	5	$100
Printing	$50	1	$50
Total Basic Budget			**$515**

BIG BUDGET

Line Item	Cost/Each	# of Each	Total Cost
Membership	$300	1	$300
Conferences	$500	1	$500
Certification Test	$150	1	$150
Test Prep Course	$500	1	$500
Other #1:			
Other #2:			
Total Big Budget			**$1,450**

1.5 HOW TO CALCULATE YOUR CURRENT PROFESSIONAL VELOCITY

Video Time: 6 minutes
Activity Time: 15 minutes

Required Tools:
- calculator

Language:
Professional Velocity = The rate at which you can help other organizations or individuals get from some point A to some point B. It is highly correlative with one's income.

Directions:
1. Complete the worksheet to calculate your current professional velocity.

YOUR CURRENT PROFESSIONAL VELOCITY

YOUR CURRENT ANNUAL SALARY = $ **50,000**

52 WEEKS - **2** VACATION WEEKS = **50** WEEKS

= $ **1,000** PER WEEK

DIVIDED BY AVERAGE HOURS PER WEEK

50 HOURS PER WEEK

Includes travel to and from work

= $ **20** PER HOUR

DIVIDED BY 60 MINUTES

= $ **0.33** PER MINUTE

DIVIDED BY 60 SECONDS

= $ **0.0055** PER SECOND

NOTE: This only assumes income generated from you working. It does not account for passive income from other assets such as real estate, stocks, or mutual funds.

www.CareerChangeChallenge.com

YOUR CURRENT PROFESSIONAL VELOCITY

YOUR CURRENT ANNUAL SALARY = $_____

52 WEEKS - ____ VACATION WEEKS = _____ **WEEKS**

= $_____ **PER WEEK**

DIVIDED BY AVERAGE HOURS PER WEEK

_____ **HOURS PER WEEK**
Includes travel to and from work

= $_____ **PER HOUR**

DIVIDED BY 60 MINUTES

= $_____ **PER MINUTE**

DIVIDED BY 60 SECONDS

= $_____ **PER SECOND**

NOTE: This only assumes income generated from you working. It does not account for passive income from other assets such as real estate, stocks, or mutual funds.

www.CareerChangeChallenge.com

1.5 HOW TO CALCULATE YOUR DESIRED PROFESSIONAL VELOCITY

Video Time: 6 minutes
Activity Time: 10 minutes

Required Tools:
- calculator

Language:
Professional Velocity = The rate at which you can help other organizations or individuals get from some point A to some point B. It is highly correlated with one's income.

Directions:
1. Declare your desired salary using your MINIMUM FROM BEFORE as a base.
2. Complete the worksheet to calculate your desired professional velocity.

YOUR DESIRED PROFESSIONAL VELOCITY

$$\frac{\text{YOUR DESIRED ANNUAL SALARY} = \$\ 200{,}000}{52\ \text{WEEKS} - \underline{12}\ \text{VACATION WEEKS} = \underline{40}\ \textbf{WEEKS}}$$

= $ _____5,000_____ **PER WEEK**

DIVIDED BY AVERAGE HOURS PER WEEK

_____50_____ **HOURS PER WEEK**
Includes travel to and from work

= $ _____100_____ **PER HOUR**

DIVIDED BY 60 MINUTES

= $ _____1.67_____ **PER MINUTE**

DIVIDED BY 60 SECONDS

= $ _____0.03_____ **PER SECOND**

NOTE: This only assumes income generated from you working. It does not account for passive income from other assets such as real estate, stocks, or mutual funds.

www.CareerChangeChallenge.com   35   Copyright © 2010 Jullien Gordon

YOUR DESIRED PROFESSIONAL VELOCITY

YOUR DESIRED ANNUAL SALARY = $ _____

52 WEEKS - ____ VACATION WEEKS = _____ **WEEKS**

= $ _____ **PER WEEK**

DIVIDED BY AVERAGE HOURS PER WEEK

_____ **HOURS PER WEEK**

Includes travel to and from work

= $ _____ **PER HOUR**

DIVIDED BY 60 MINUTES

= $ _____ **PER MINUTE**

DIVIDED BY 60 SECONDS

= $ _____ **PER SECOND**

NOTE: This only assumes income generated from you working. It does not account for passive income from other assets such as real estate, stocks, or mutual funds.

1.6 HOW TO OVERCOME OTHER BARRIERS TO EXIT

Video Time: 5 minutes
Activity Time: 30 minutes

Required Tools:
None

Language:
SWOT Analysis = Strengths Weakness Threats & Opportunities assessment

Directions:
1. Consider your personal, intellectual, social, and financial capital and the questions associated with each one and write where you have strengths in the first box on the top row (e.g. strong communicator, $20,000 saved up, diverse network in finance, etc).
2. Consider your personal, intellectual, social, and financial capital and the questions associated with each one and write where you have weakness in the second box on the top row (e.g. no connections in the industry, only know one language, $80K in debt, job hopping since college, etc).
3. Given your strengths and capital write what opportunities are on your horizon based on your strengths in box one in the second row (e.g. start a marketing company with Billy, move to California's booming Silicon Valley, join Acme's product development team, go back and get my JD/MBA).
4. Given your weaknesses and lack of capital write what threats are on your horizon based on your weaknesses in box two in the second row (i.e. industry shifting toward automation, jobs being outsourced, my skills are becoming less relevant every day).

SWOT Analysis Questions to Consider

STRENGTHS	WEAKNESSES

Personal Capital
- What are your personal strengths?
- What are your professional strengths?
- What are your passions?

Intellectual Capital
- What skills or subjects do you claim to be an expert at?
- What certificates, licenses, degrees, or trainings have you completed?
- What other languages do you know? Spanish? HTML? PHP?

Social Capital
- Name 10 older people who can help you.
- Who are your professional mentors?
- What local and national professional organizations are you connected to?

Financial Capital
- How much financial freedom do you have?
- Do you have other sources of income besides your paycheck?
- How much liquid assets do you have?

OPPORTUNITIES	THREATS

Personal
- How many dependents do you have?
- How willing is your family to endure your career change?
- How is your physical, mental, and emotional health?
- What have you been studying, reading, and learning to stay ahead of the curve?

Industry
- What trends do you see in your industry that are working for or against you?
- Is your industry growing or fading? Would you invest money in it today?
- What new innovations are on the horizon that can destroy or resurrect your industry?
- How many people do you know at companies that interest you?
- What have your created or done that has been extremely valuable in the past 3 years?

Local, National, & Global
- What trends do you see locally, nationally, or globally around the world that are working for or against you?

SWOT Analysis

STRENGTHS	WEAKNESSES

OPPORTUNITIES	THREATS

DAY 03

1.7 HOW TO CREATE YOUR PERSONAL SUCCESS DASHBOARD

Video Time: 3 minutes
Activity Time: 30 minutes

Required Tools:
None

Language:
Dashboard = a way to measure your progress toward your D.R.E.A.M. even if only correlative

Directions:
1. Complete your personal success statements.
2. Complete your professional success statements.

DASHBOARDS

PERSONAL SUCCESS STATEMENTS

Directions: Fill in the frequency, action verb, and measurement for the three personal success statements below.

Example:

By the end *of my life*, I want to have *inspired* *1,000,000*
                  Frequency   Action Verb   Quantity

people to live more purpose-filled lives
                      Area of Measurement

1. By the end ...., I want to have ....
                  Frequency   Action Verb   Quantity

....
                      Area of Measurement

2. By the end ...., I want to have ....
                  Frequency   Action Verb   Quantity

....
                      Area of Measurement

3. By the end ...., I want to have ....
                  Frequency   Action Verb   Quantity

....
                      Area of Measurement

Professions Related to My Personal Dashboard Include:........................

....

DASHBOARDS

PROFESSIONAL SUCCESS STATEMENTS

Directions: Fill in the frequency, action verb, and measurement for the three personal success statements below.

Example:

By the end ...., I want to have ....
                     Frequency   Action Verb   Quantity

....
                                             Area of Measurement

1. By the end ...., I want to have ....
                     Frequency   Action Verb   Quantity

....
                                             Area of Measurement

2. By the end ...., I want to have ....
                     Frequency   Action Verb   Quantity

....
                                             Area of Measurement

3. By the end ...., I want to have ....
                     Frequency   Action Verb   Quantity

....
                                             Area of Measurement

Professions Related to My Professional Dashboard Include:...........................

....

DASHBOARDS

Directions: Based on the metrics of success you created above, use the space below to draw a visual representation of your dashboard like you are in a vehicle.

1.8 HOW TO IDENTIFY YOUR PASSIONS

Video Time: 11 minutes
Activity Time: 60 minutes

Required Tools:
None

Language:
None

Directions:
1. List all of your favorites in column 1 of each section.
2. In column 2, list up 3 passions that that activity or item might have been speaking to in you.
3. In column 3, look at each passion in column 2 individually and then list a career path that connects with that passion.
4. Based on your answers, identify the top 3 passions you wouldn't mind using for the rest of your life.
5. Based on your answers, identify 3 professional paths that you are interested in exploring further.

PASSION FINDER

Directions: Complete the chart below with your favorite things and their associated passions. Finally, weave together the various passions to create a one sentence passion statement that is unique to you.

MY FAVORITE BOOK IS...	THIS SPEAKS TO MY PASSION FOR...	CAREER PATHS THAT CONNECT ARE...
THE ALCHEMIST	SEEKING TRUTH	MINISTER
	LEARNING FROM LIFE	ANTHROPOLOGIST
	FINDNG SELF	MONK

MY FAVORITE THING TO DO ALONE IS...	THIS SPEAKS TO MY PASSION FOR...	CAREER PATHS THAT CONNECT ARE...

MY FAVORITE THING TO DO WITH OTHERS IS...	THIS SPEAKS TO MY PASSION FOR...	CAREER PATHS THAT CONNECT ARE...

MY FAVORITE THING TO DO AT WORK IS...	THIS SPEAKS TO MY PASSION FOR...	CAREER PATHS THAT CONNECT ARE...

MY FAVORITE SUBJECT IN SCHOOL IS/WAS...	THIS SPEAKS TO MY PASSION FOR...	CAREER PATHS THAT CONNECT ARE...

MY FAVORITE SUBJECT OUT OF SCHOOL IS...	THIS SPEAKS TO MY PASSION FOR...	CAREER PATHS THAT CONNECT ARE...

MY FAVORITE TV SHOW IS...	THIS SPEAKS TO MY PASSION FOR...	CAREER PATHS THAT CONNECT ARE...

MY FAVORITE BOOK IS...	THIS SPEAKS TO MY PASSION FOR...	CAREER PATHS THAT CONNECT ARE...

MY FAVORITE MOVIE IS...	THIS SPEAKS TO MY PASSION FOR...	CAREER PATHS THAT CONNECT ARE...

MY FAVORITE WEBSITE IS...	THIS SPEAKS TO MY PASSION FOR...	CAREER PATHS THAT CONNECT ARE...

MY FAVORITE SUPERHERO OR CARTOON CHARACTER IS...	THIS SPEAKS TO MY PASSION FOR...	CAREER PATHS THAT CONNECT ARE...

MY FAVORITE PRODUCT IS...	THIS SPEAKS TO MY PASSION FOR...	CAREER PATHS THAT CONNECT ARE...

MY FAVORITE COMPANY IS...	THIS SPEAKS TO MY PASSION FOR...	CAREER PATHS THAT CONNECT ARE...

MY FAVORITE NON-PROFIT ORGANIZATION IS...	THIS SPEAKS TO MY PASSION FOR...	CAREER PATHS THAT CONNECT ARE...

MY FAVORITE VIDEO OR BOARD GAME...	THIS SPEAKS TO MY PASSION FOR...	CAREER PATHS THAT CONNECT ARE...

MY FAVORITE MUSICIAN...	THIS SPEAKS TO MY PASSION FOR...	CAREER PATHS THAT CONNECT ARE...

MY FAVORITE SPORT...	THIS SPEAKS TO MY PASSION FOR...	CAREER PATHS THAT CONNECT ARE...

The Passions That Came Up The Most Include:

1. ....

2. ....

3. ....

The Professional Paths I Want To Explore More include:

1. ....

2. ....

3. ....

DAY 04

1.9 HOW TO IDENTIFY A PROBLEM THAT MATTERS TO YOU

Video Time: 7 minutes
Activity Time: 35 minutes

Required Tools:
None

Language:
None

Directions:
1. List all of the personal pain & gain points that come to mind based on the prompts.
2. List all of the professional pain & gain points that come to mind based on the prompts.
3. Choose the top 3 that you could see yourself dedicating your life to solving.
4. Identify related professions that would allow you to solve those problems daily.

INNER TERM-OIL

Directions: Think of problems you see in the lives of your family, friends, company, and community. Complete the following charts for your personal and professional life to explore the problems that are currently present in your life and around you. Observe any patterns in the types of problems you see.

Personal Pain & Gain Points:

Problems I have faced in my life:..

....

Problems others close to me are facing:...

....

Social Problems:

Social problems that make me mad/sad:..

....

Causes I've donated to or volunteered for:..

....

Creative Questions:

If I had one wish, I would put an end to the problem of:..........................

....

Business ideas I've thought but not acted on:...

....

Related Professions Include:...

....

Professional Pain & Gain Points:

Customers Needs:

The 3 biggest problems I hear our customers mention about *their business* are:

1. ....

2. ....

3. ....

Products & Services:

The 3 biggest problems I hear our customers mention about *our products/ services* are:

1. ....

2. ....

3. ....

Company Culture & Processes:

The 3 biggest problems I hear my colleagues mention about *our company* are:

1. ....

2. ....

3. ....

Related Professions Include:..

....

The Problems That Matter Most To Me:

I could see myself dedicating my life to solving either of the following problems:

1...

2...

3...

Related Professions Include:...

....

1.10 HOW TO IDENTIFY YOUR TARGET MARKET

Video Time: 3 minutes
Activity Time: 20 minutes

Required Tools:
None

Language:
None

Directions:
1. Think about who you want to help and how.
2. Put yourself in the shoes of your end customer or colleagues and complete the testimony.

CUSTOMER/CLIENT TESTIMONY

Directions: Write the autobiography of whom you want to serve. Address where they are on their journey when you meet, how you want to serve them, and where they end up as a result of your service. Create the character or pull from a true story.

My name is (Customer Name)..and I was initially in

a state of ....

....

....

Before I met (Your Name)..., I was [] stuck & not going anywhere [] broken & not going fast enough [] lost & not going the right way. On my own, it was impossible for me to reach my desired state, which is

....

....

(Your Name) .... helped me get there by (What you did)

....

....

....

....

....

As a result of his/her contribution, it is now possible for me to

....

....

This profound change in my life allows me to use my vehicle to positively impact (Who they serve)..

....

10 PROFESSIONAL PATHS WHERE THIS STORY MAY COME TRUE

....	....
....	....
....	....
....	....
....	....

1.11 HOW TO FIND YOUR NICHE & POSITION YOURSELF TO WIN

Video Time: 7 minutes
Activity Time: 40 minutes

Required Tools:
None

Language:
None

Directions:
1. Set a timer for 5 minutes and then try to come up with a career path for each letter of the alphabet.
2. Declare your commitment to be the world's greatest at something and identify a corresponding superhero name based on your commitment.
3. Identify 3 powers or skills that you must practice and develop to become the best.
4. Create two routines for each skill that you will integrate into your daily life.

A-Z CAREER PATHS

Directions: Write down a potential career path for each letter of the alphabet. Be as original and innovative as possible. Time yourself with a stop watch.

A		N	
B		O	
C		P	
D		Q	
E		R	
F		S	
G		T	
H		U	
I		V	
J		W	
K		X	
L		Y	
M		Z	

How long did it take you? _____ : _____
                                          MIN   SEC

Find lots of answers at: http://www.bls.gov/oes/current/oes_alph.htm

CHOOSE OR CREATE A SUPER HERO NAME

Person	Super Hero Name	Super Power
Caesar Milan	Dog Whisper	The power to connect with dogs and train them to behave
Troy Dunn	The Locator	The power to help people locate long lost family members
Jesus	Christ (Anointed One)	The power to anoint people
Muhammad Yunus	Banker to the Poor	The power to create innovative financial models to empower entrepreneurs
Oscar Pistorius	Blade Runner	The power to run extremely fast with prosthetic legs
Steve Irwin	The Crocodile Hunter	The power to tame crocodiles and other animals
Stephen Wlitshire	The Human Camera	The power to capture complex images in his head (ie the entire birds-eye view of a city) and then draw it from memory despite having autism.

What are your nicknames from childhood? sports? family? friends?

....

....

What are potential names based on your passions?
Example: The Connector for someone who is passionate about connecting people

....

....

What are potential names based on your problems?
Example: The Healer for someone who wants to alleviate pain in the world

....

....

My super hero name is:..

Example Names

The Advocate

bReignStorm

CEO

Charlie the Great

The Clenched Fist

Coach

The Connector

The Conscious Hustla

The Chancellor

Correspondence

The Creator

D-Smoke

Deus Style

Don Milagro/Mr. Miracle

DopeSwan

Dr. Grow

Dream Catcher

Elevator

The Enlightener

E-Train

The Explorer

Exposure

The Gatekeeper

Ghetto Man the Prophet

Ghost Speaker

Heavenly Glory

The Justice

The Innovator

Kali Kenetic Educator

Lady Godiva the Communicator

The Life Guard

The Mayor

Melody Moses

The Mirror

Mr. Ezquire

The Music Making Do Gooder

The Negotiator

Nikki Numbers

Oakademy

Potential Pusher

The Prophet

Reflector

Sharp Shooter

Show Time

Storyteller

Superbeene the Builder

The Sythesizer

The Third-Eye Transformer

Truth Bearer

Truth Seeker

Poetic Soul

Poverty Killer

La Veritas

Voice of the Go Getter

The Warden

Well-Nes

Wellness Guru

Yo-Vision

CONCRETE PLANS & ROUTINES

Directions: Create a super hero name for yourself and define what you want to be the world's best at doing. List 3 super powers, skills, strengths, or abilities connected to your name and positioning. Come up with two **routines (a set of daily, weekly, or monthly actions to maintain progress)**. Your superhero should be consistent in your personal and professional life.

Commitment: To be the world's best at helping people find their purpose & make a living doing what they love

Super Hero Name: The Purpose Finder

Example Power: Ability to inspire people instantaneously

Routine E.1: Create conversations about life with 2 or more people weekly

Routine E.2: Read inspirational text for 30 minutes daily = 3.5 hours/week

I'm committed to being the world's best at: ....

....

Super Hero Name: ....

Power #1: ....

Routine 1.1: ....

I will do this .... times/day or .... times/week, which equals .... hr/week

Routine 1.2: ....

I will do this .... times/day or .... times/week, which equals .... hr/week

Related Professions Include: ....

....

Power #2:..

Routine 2.1:..

I will do this .... times/day or .... times/week, which equals .... hr/week

Routine 2.2:..

I will do this .... times/day or .... times/week, which equals .... hr/week

Related Professions Include:...

....

Power #3:..

Routine 3.1:..

I will do this .... times/day or .... times/week, which equals .... hr/week

Routine 3.2:..

I will do this .... times/day or .... times/week, which equals .... hr/week

Related Professions Include:...

....

DAY 05

1.12 HOW TO THINK LIKE A CAREER PIONEER

Video Time: 10 minutes
Activity Time: 40 minutes

Required Tools:
None

Language:
None

Directions:
1. Name 3 personal pioneers and 3 professional pioneers and list the career/jobs they had during their lifetime.
2. Write a thank you note to one of your personal pioneers expressing why you think they are a pioneer, and how they change you and the world through their journey. They can be alive or deceased or an individual or an organization. If they are an individual who is alive, I encourage you to send it to them.
3. Choose one of your professional pioneers and consider their path. Where was your industry when they began, what they did that was new, and where you hope to take it after they stop.
4. List up to 4 assumptions or old beliefs you see in your industry and articulate your alternative viewpoint.

MY PERSONAL & PROFESSIONAL PIONEERS

Personal Pioneers	Careers/Jobs They Had
1	
2	
3	
Professional Pioneers	**Careers/Jobs They Had**
1	
2	
3	

PERSONAL PIONEERS

Interview at least one of your personal pioneers. Before going inside them, tell them why you chose to interview them and what you admire about them from the outside looking in.

CAREER QUEST-IONNAIRE

- What did you think you were going to be when you grew up?

- How did that change and evolve over time?

- Do you love what you do now?

- In your eyes, what questions should I be asking myself as I navigate my career change?

- What tradeoffs have you had to make along the way regarding your time, family, and money?

- How much does it cost to maintain your current lifestyle?

- If you could do it all over again, (if anything) what would you do differently?

- I've discovered that I'm passionate about _____. Do you have any ideas about where I could apply this passion or any connections to people you think I should talk to?

PROFESSIONAL PIONEERS

Directions: Identify one of your path-specific pioneers and the lanes they occupied and map out where they began, where they ended, and how you plan to take it further. Secondly, list some assumptions from your lane or industry and write alter-native viewpoints that challenge the old way of thinking.

Pioneer Name:..

Lane/Industry/Skill:...

Where did the lane end when they started?

....

....

....

Where and how did they pave a new road?

....

....

....

Where and how do you envision taking the road further?

....

....

....

....

ASSUMPTIONS & ALTERNATIVES

ASSUMPTIONS/ RULES IN MY LANE	ALTERNATIVE/ CHALLENGING VIEWPOINTS
Example: Personal development is personal	*Example: Personal development works best in groups*
Assumption 1	Alter-native Viewpoint 1
Assumption 2	Alter-native Viewpoint 2
Assumption 3	Alter-native Viewpoint 3
Assumption 4	Alter-native Viewpoint 4

1.13 HOW TO CREATE YOUR CAREER VISION

Video Time: 8 minutes
Activity Time: 30 minutes

Required Tools:
- poster board
- glue stick
- scissors
- magazines

Language:
Visioning = the process of forecasting your future using your imagination, words, and images

Directions:
1. Imagine that you are at your funeral or 80th birthday and your best friend is going to say a eulogy or a toast. Write a short speech of what you would want him or her to say about your CHARACTER at that moment.
2. Imagine that you are at your retirement party on the last day of your work. Friends, family, kids, and colleagues are present. Write a short retirement speech about your CAREER and its meaning whatever company you're with and the people it served and its impact on the world.

EULOGY OR TOAST

Directions: Write a eulogy or a toast to yourself from the perspective of your best friend when you're 80 years old. Questions to consider include:

- What roles do I envision myself taking on throughout my life? (i.e. parent, community leader, entrepreneur)
- What do I hope to leave behind? (i.e. family business, lasting change, my art, legacy)
- What's one word, belief, or quote that people will remember me for? Why? (i.e. honest, authentic, inspirational)

RE-TIRE-MEANT SPEECH

Directions: Imagine the last day of your career after 40 years of hard work. Finally, retirement! Write a short speech outlining the value you created, the legacy you left, the lives you impacted, the growth you sparked and experienced, and the change you brought about in your organization(s), industry, and world.

...... years and .... months from today, ..., ..., 20.....

....

....

....

....

....

....

....

....

....

....

....

....

....

Other Related Professions Include:...

....

DAY 06

1.14 HOW TO LEAVE A LEGACY

Video Time: 5 minutes
Activity Time: 20 minutes

Required Tools:
None

Language:
4 Ways to Leave a Legacy = Baby Bodies, Bodies of Work, Institutional Bodies, Your Body in Service to Others

Directions:
1. Use the prompts to consider what will be possible in the lives of those you touch personally because of you that would not possible without you.
2. Use the prompts to consider what will be possible in the lives of those you touch professionally because of you that would not possible without you.

4 WAYS TO LEAVE YOUR LEGACY

Directions: Write the name/title of the body you intend to leave and the year you intend to create it.

1. Baby Bodies

....Year ....

....Year ....

....Year ....

....Year ....

....Year ....

2. Bodies of Work

....Year ....

....Year ....

....Year ....

....Year ....

....Year ....

3. Institutional Bodies

....Year ....

....Year ....

....Year ....

....Year ....

....Year ....

4 WAYS TO LEAVE YOUR LEGACY

Directions: Write your eulogy again from the perspective of your best friend without mentioning anything from the other 3 bodies.

4. Body in Service to Others

IN-POSSIBILITY

Directions: Complete the following statements for your personal life based on the new possibilities you want to see for the different people you touch with your presence and actions.

Because of my personal life….

…my family will be able to…

………………………………………………………………………………………………………

………………………………………………………………………………………………………

………………………………………………………………………………………………………

…my friends will be able to…

………………………………………………………………………………………………………

………………………………………………………………………………………………………

………………………………………………………………………………………………………

…my community will be able to…

………………………………………………………………………………………………………

………………………………………………………………………………………………………

………………………………………………………………………………………………………

…my world will be able to…

………………………………………………………………………………………………………

………………………………………………………………………………………………………

………………………………………………………………………………………………………

IN-POSSIBILITY

Directions: Complete the following statements for your professional life based on the new possibilities you want to see for the different people you touch with your presence and actions.

Because of my professional life….

…my customers will be able to…

....

....

....

…my company will be able to…

....

....

....

…my colleagues will be able to…

....

....

....

…my industry will be able to…

....

....

....

1.15 HOW TO CREATE YOUR 30 SECOND PITCH

Video Time: 5 minutes
Activity Time: 15 minutes

Required Tools:
- voice recorder (optional)

Language:
None

Directions:
1. Use the template and your answers from the 8 Cylinders of Success to create your 30 second pitch.
2. Commit it to memory by rehearsing it.

MY 30 SECOND PITCH

Directions: Now that you've finished reading the book and have a bit more clarity on your 8 Cylinders of Success, write your new purpose statement using keywords and phrases from your worksheets. You can use the purpose statement template provided below or write it in free form. When you're done, compare it to your first purpose statement and see if you hear or feel a difference.

30 SECOND PITCH EXAMPLE

My name is *Jullien Gordon* and I'm a *PurposeFinder*
            YOUR NAME   YOUR POSITIONING OR SUPER HERO NAME

My work makes it possible for *people who hate their jobs*
                                      YOUR PEOPLE OR TARGET MARKET

to address *underemployment, unemployment, overwork, & underpay*
                            YOUR PROBLEM OR PAIN/GAIN POINT

and experience/achieve *what it means to D.R.E.A.M awake*
                                YOUR POSSIBILITY

I have a *Tony Robbins*-like passion for
                YOUR PIONEER

helping people grow and create the life they always dreamed of
                                 YOUR PASSION

and I envision a world where *everyone makes their highest contribution*
                                              YOUR PICTURE

www.CareerChangeChallenge.com

30 SECOND PITCH TEMPLATE

My name is .... and I'm a ....
                   YOUR NAME   YOUR POSITIONING OR SUPER HERO NAME

My work makes it possible for ....
                                              YOUR PEOPLE OR TARGET MARKET

to address...
                                YOUR PROBLEM OR PAIN/GAIN POINT

and experience/achieve...
                                            YOUR POSSIBILITY

I have a ....-like passion for..
               YOUR PIONEER

....
                                            YOUR PASSION

and I envision a world where...
                                              YOUR PICTURE

FREE FORM 30 SECOND PITCH

My name is .... and I'm a ....
                 YOUR NAME   SUPER HERO NAME

....

....

....

....

....

....

....

1.16 HOW TO MEASURE YOUR ALIGNMENT WITH YOUR EXISTING COMPANY

Video Time: 8 minutes
Activity Time: 45 minutes

Required Tools:
None

Language:
None

Directions:
1. Now that you've completed your personal 8 Cylinders of Success, assess the 8 Cylinders of Success for your company and/or department/division and write down the answers.
2. Check the boxes according to how aligned you feel with your company and simply observe the areas where you are aligned and misaligned.

THE 8 CYLINDERS OF SUCCESS - PERSONAL

Part 1		Where am I?
Principles	Your Dashboard	What beliefs equate to success to me?
Passions	Your Keys	What do I love doing and why?
Problems	Your Fuel	What social, scientific, technical, or personal problem do I want to solve?
People	Your Motor	Who moves you to want to serve them and in what way?

Part 2		Where am I going?
Positioning	Your Lane	What do I want to be #1 in the world at?
Pioneers	Your Pace Cars	Who are my models, mentors, and guides?
Picture	Your Road Map	What's my vision for myself and my world?
Possibility	Your Destination	What's possible in the world *with* me that would not be possible *without* me?

THE 8 CYLINDERS OF SUCCESS - PROFESSIONAL

Part 1		Where are we?
Principles	My Company's Dashboard	What are my company's values and metrics for success? How is my success measured here?
Passions	My Company's Keys	What are my company's competitive advantages and strengths? What strengths am I exercising and developing while at my company?
Problems	My Company's Fuel	What is my company's customers' personal, social, scientific, or technical problem? What related problems do I get to solve?
People	My Company's Motor	Who is my company's target market or customer? Who do I serve to ensure that the end customer receives quality service?
Part 2		Where are we going?
Positioning	My Company's Lane	What business or industry does my company want to establish itself as a leader? What is my career positioning me to be great at doing?
Pioneers	My Company's Pace Cars	Who are the old and new industry leaders? How is my position helping us be an industry leader?
Picture	My Company's Road Map	What's my company's vision for our organization and the world? What's my company's vision for my career?
Possibility	My Company's Destination	What's possible in the world with my company that would not be possible without it? What is or will be possible for my company that wasn't possible before me?

www.CareerChangeChallenge.com   Copyright © 2010 Jullien Gordon

My company's answers (see website, annual reports, or pull from experience)

My company's answers (see website, annual reports, or pull from experience)

PURPOSE & PROFESSIONAL ALIGNMENT

	EVERY DAY	SOMETIMES	NEVER
PRINCIPLES			
MY CONSCIOUS IS FREE AT & AFTER WORK			
I CAN IMPROVE MY DASHBOARD HERE			
PASSIONS			
I'M ABLE TO USE MY PASSIONS HERE			
MY WORK HOURS ALLOW ME TO ENJOY LIFE			
PROBLEMS			
I SOLVE MEANINGFUL PROBLEMS HERE			
PEOPLE			
I SERVE PEOPLE I CARE ABOUT HERE			
POSITIONING			
I'M ACHIEVING MASTERY AT A SKILL HERE			
I FEEL THEY ARE INVESTED IN MY SUCCESS			
PIONEERS			
I HAVE GREAT MENTORS HERE			
I'M DEVELOPING ALL 4 CAPITALS HERE			
I LEARN A LOT FROM PEOPLE ABOVE ME			
PICTURE			
MY WORK IS ALIGNED WITH MY LIFE VISION			
I'M ALLOWED TO CREATE HERE			
POSSIBILITY			
I FEEL LIKE WE'RE CHANGING THE WORLD			
PEOPLE WOULD HURT IF WE WEREN'T HERE			

DAY 07

1.17 HOW TO EVALUATE WHAT ACTIVITIES FULFILL YOU AND DEPLETE YOU

Video Time: 4 minutes
Activity Time: 20 minutes

Required Tools:
None

Language:
None

Directions:
1. List all of the actions your job involves weekly
2. Estimate how many hours per week you spend doing each action in column 2.
3. If that action fulfills you, write the same number is column 3. If it depletes you, write the number is column 4.
4. Add up the total hours account for line item for columns 2, 3, and 4.
5. Divide the # of fulfilled hours by the total hours to get the percentage of time you are fulfilled at work.
6. Divide the # of depleted hours by the total hours to get the percentage of time you are depleted at work.

TOP 20 WEEKLY PROFESSIONAL ACTIONS	HOURS	FULFILL	DEPLETE
1			
2			
3			
4			
5			
6			
7			
8			
9			
10			
11			
12			
13			
14			
15			
16			
17			
18			
19			
20			
21 TRAVEL TO & FROM WORK			
TOTAL HOURS ACCOUNTED FOR			
PERCENTAGE		%	%

1.18 HOW TO MAKE SURE YOU DON'T REPEAT THE SAME MISTAKE TWICE

Video Time: 5 minutes
Activity Time: 60 minutes

Required Tools:
None

Language:
None

Directions:
1. List your current job title.
2. List your top 3 reasons why you chose this job.
3. Let go of your existing job title and for each reason you chose the job, write down up to two other career paths that would allow you to get this.
4. List the top 3 things missing from this job.
5. For each thing missing from your current job, list two career paths that could get you what you are looking for.
6. Evaluate your last job search by checking off everything you used on the list and then answering the questions.

My Current Job: _____

TOP 3 REASONS I CHOSE THIS JOB	OTHER CAREER PATHS THAT WOULD ALSO GET ME THIS
1	
2	
3	

TOP 3 THINGS NOT AT THIS JOB	OTHER CAREER PATHS THAT COULD GET ME THIS INSTEAD
1	
2	
3	

PEOPLE
[] Friends
[] Colleagues
[] Mentors
[] Old Boss
[] Parents
[] Neighbors
[] Old Classmates
[] Parents or Siblings
[] Extended Family
[] Reached out to strangers
[] Hired a recruiter
[] Career or life coach

MEALS
[] Met people for coffee
[] Took people to lunch
[] Took people to dinner

COMMUNICATIONS
[] In person
[] Phone
[] Direct Mail
[] Email
[] Facebook Messages or Wall Posts
[] Twitter
[] LinkedIn Messages

PLACES
[] Undergrad Career/Alumni Services
[] Grad School Career/Alumni Services
[] The Public Library

EVENTS
[] Job Fairs
[] Networking Events
[] Informational Interviews
[] Info Sessions

TOOLS
[] Business cards
[] Business card holder
[] Padfolio

WEBSITES FOR SEARCH
[] Monster.com
[] CareerBuilder.com
[] HotJobs.com
[] SimplyHired.com

[] Indeed.com
[] Idealist.org
[] Craigslist.org
[] Company websites
[] Newspapers (online or physical)

MY ONLINE PRESENCE
[] Used LinkedIn.com
[] Used Facebook.com
[] Had people write recommendations
[] Created my own website
[] Started industry-related blogging

DOCUMENTS
[] Updated my resume
[] Updated my cover letter
[] Got letters of recommendation
[] Create a portfolio of my past work
[] Created a resume 2.0
[] Certificate or License
[] Standardized Test Score (i.e. GMAT)
[] Graduate or undergraduate degree

SELF ASSESSMENT
[] Strengths Finder 2.0
[] Myers-Briggs
[] Bought Career-related books
[] Took time off

RESEARCH
[] Vault.com
[] Internship
[] Info Session
[] Talked to current employees
[] Talked to former employees
[] Annual report (if public)

FOLLOW UP
[] Thank you email
[] Mailed thank you card

NEGOTIATION
[] Researched competitive salaries

Please list any other resources, relationships, or actions you took to land your current job:

....

....

....

What do you want to do differently to ensure you don't repeat the same mistake?

....

....

....

....

What assumptions did you make last time that you want to avoid this time?

....

....

....

....

What questions do you want to ask yourself or potential employer early on this time?

....

....

....

....

....

DAY 08

D.R.E.A.M.

=

DESIRED

RELATIONSHIPS

EMPLOYMENT

AND

MONEY

1.19 HOW TO ASSESS YOUR CURRENT SKILL SET

Video Time: 9 minutes
Activity Time: 60 minutes

Required Tools:
None

Language:
Intellectual Capital = The skills or subjects that you are way above average in/at
Skill = an action by which someone can replicate success more frequently than the average person

Directions:
1. Create a list of 20 things you know how to do well.
2. Mark if someone you enjoy doing the activity and if someone gets paid to do it.
3. List the top two professional skills associated with the task.
4. Mark if someone gets paid full-time to do the activity.
5. List the career paths related to the skill.

SOME SKILLS TO CONSIDER

- administering programs
- planning agendas/meetings
- updating files
- advising people
- planning organizational needs
- setting up demonstrations
- analyzing data
- predicting futures
- sketching charts or diagrams
- assembling apparatus
- rehabilitating people
- writing reports
- auditing financial reports
- organizing tasks
- writing for publication
- budgeting expenses
- prioritizing work
- expressing feelings
- calculating numerical data
- creating new ideas
- checking for accuracy
- finding information
- meeting people
- classifying records
- handling complaints
- evaluating programs
- coaching individuals
- handling detail work
- editing work
- collecting money
- imagining new solutions
- tolerating interruptions
- compiling statistics
- interpreting languages
- confronting other people
- inventing new ideas
- dispensing information
- constructing buildings
- proposing ideas
- adapting new procedures
- coping with deadlines
- investigating problems
- negotiating/arbitrating conflicts promoting events
- locating missing information
- speaking to the public
- raising funds
- dramatizing ideas
- writing letters/papers/proposals questioning others
- estimating physical space
- reading volumes of material
- being thorough
- organizing files
- remembering information
- coordinating schedules/times managing people
- interviewing prospective employees running meetings
- selling products
- listening to others
- supervising employees
- teaching/instructing/training individuals
- relating to the public
- enduring long hours
- inspecting physical objects
- entertaining people
- displaying artistic ideas
- distributing products
- deciding uses of money
- managing an organization
- delegating responsibility
- measuring boundaries
- serving individuals
- mediating between people
- counseling/consulting people
- motivating others
- persuading others
- operating equipment
- reporting information
- summarizing information
- supporting others
- encouraging others
- delegating responsibilities
- determining a problem
- defining a problem
- comparing results
- screening telephone calls
- maintaining accurate records
- drafting reports
- collaborating ideas administering medication comprehending ideas
- overseeing operations motivating others
- generating accounts
- teaching/instructing/training individuals
- thinking in a logical manner making decisions
- becoming actively involved defining performance standards resolving conflicts
- analyzing problems recommending courses of action
- selling ideas
- preparing written communications
- expressing ideas orally to individuals or groups conducting interviews
- performing numeric analysis conducting meetings
- setting priorities
- setting work/committee goals developing plans for projects gathering information
- taking personal responsibility thinking of creative ideas providing discipline when necessary
- maintaining a high level of activity
- enforcing rules and regulations
- meeting new people
- developing a climate of enthusiasm, teamwork, and cooperation
- interacting with people at different levels
- picking out important information
- creating meaningful and challenging work
- taking independent action skillfully applying professional knowledge
- maintaining emotional control under stress
- knowledge of concepts and principles
- providing customers with service
- knowledge of community/ government affairs

I KNOW HOW TO... (NOTE: DON'T USE "HELP" AS YOUR STARTER VERB. IT'S TOO VAGUE.)	LIST THE JOB, EVENT, CLIENT, OR STORY YOU HAVE TO TELL ABOUT THIS SKILL
EX. *Get people motivated to move*	*Route 66 Tour*
1	
2	
3	
4	
5	
6	
7	
8	
9	
10	
11	
12	
13	
14	
15	
16	
17	
18	
19	
20	

POINT A: WHERE AN INDIVIDUAL, ORGANIZATION, OR THING WAS BEFORE	POINT B: WHERE AN INDIVIDUAL, ORGANIZATION, OR THING WAS AFTER
unmotivated, depressed, stuck	*motivated, alive, in motion*
1	
2	
3	
4	
5	
6	
7	
8	
9	
10	
11	
12	
13	
14	
15	
16	
17	
18	
19	
20	

I KNOW HOW TO... (NOTE: DON'T USE "HELP" AS YOUR STARTER VERB. IT'S TOO VAGUE.)	LIST THE JOB, EVENT, CLIENT, OR STORY YOU HAVE TO TELL ABOUT THIS SKILL
EX. *Get people motivated to move*	*Route 66 Tour*
1	
2	
3	
4	
5	
6	
7	
8	
9	
10	
11	
12	
13	
14	
15	
16	
17	
18	
19	
20	

DO YOU LIKE THIS ACTION?	REVERSE SKILLS INVENTORY: SKILLS THAT DEFINE THIS HOW-TO OR THAT ARE REQUIRED TO SUCCEED AT THIS ACTION	CAREER PATHS THAT REQUIRE THIS HOW-TO AND/OR SKILL SET
X	communicating with others	speaker, CEO
1		
2		
3		
4		
5		
6		
7		
8		
9		
10		
11		
12		
13		
14		
15		
16		
17		
18		
19		
20		

1.20 HOW TO SEND OUT 30 DAY DO IT RECAP EMAIL

Video Time: 2 minutes
Activity Time: 10 minutes

Required Tools:
None

Language:
None

Directions:
1. Use the email template below to engage your 30 Day Do It group in your career change process.

SUBJECT: Last Week's 30 Day Do It Recap

BODY: Hello Goal Achievers,

Last week was amazing! I'm so inspired by each of you and your goals. Thank you for blessing my home.

Our 30-Day Do It Goals are as follows:

Michelle: Read us the first chapter of her book to create momentum toward her first book

John: Lose 10 pounds and squeeze into his old jeans so that he can be a better father to his athletic kids

Jamie: Clean her garage so that she can create a home office and show us before and after pictures

Me: Meet with 15 people for at least 15 minutes via phone or in person regarding my career change

The next 30 Day Do It will be at Mike's house on October 11th at 7pm. Bring a new member and snack if you can.

When you get a chance:
1. Take my "super hero" survey
2. Forward me any job opportunities you come across

Sincerely,

Your Name

1.21 HOW TO IDENTIFY YOUR TOP 5 STRENGTHS

Video Time: 5 minutes
Activity Time: 60 minutes

Required Tools:
- Gallup StrengthsFinder 2.0 book

Language:
Personal Capital = one's awareness of their true worth and abilities through an accurate assessment of their purpose, strengths, and skills

Directions:
1. Go the bookstore and find StrengthsFinder 2.0.
2. Either buy the book, take the test and find you top 5 Strengths and read them or
3. Sit in the book store, choose the 5 that you think represent you most and reach them.

List your top 5 strengths

STRENGTH #1:..

ONE EXAMPLE OF YOU DEMONSTRATING THIS STRENGTH IN YOUR CAREER

....

....

....

STRENGTH #2:..

ONE EXAMPLE OF YOU DEMONSTRATING THIS STRENGTH IN YOUR CAREER

....

....

....

STRENGTH #3:..

ONE EXAMPLE OF YOU DEMONSTRATING THIS STRENGTH IN YOUR CAREER

....

....

....

STRENGTH #4:..

ONE EXAMPLE OF YOU DEMONSTRATING THIS STRENGTH IN YOUR CAREER

....

....

....

STRENGTH #5: ....

ONE EXAMPLE OF YOU DEMONSTRATING THIS STRENGTH IN YOUR CAREER

....

....

....

THE DUMB "WHAT'S YOUR GREATEST WEAKNESS?" QUESTIONS

CHOOSE ONE OF YOUR 5 STRENGTHS: ....

NAME THAT STRENGTH WHEN OVERUSED: ....

WRITE AN EXAMPLE OF HOW YOU OVERUSED A STRENGTH AND IT BECAME A WEAKNESS FOR THAT MOMENT

....

....

....

....

....

....

....

....

....

....

MODULE TWO

Attract Your D.R.E.A.M. Career

2.1 HOW TO GET YOUR FRIENDS' INSIGHTS ON YOUR PERSONAL BRAND

Video Time: 3 minutes
Activity Time: 15 minutes

Required Tools:
None

Language:
None

Directions:
1. Identify 5 or more friends who may be able to give you insight on who you are.
2. Cut, copy, & paste the email template below and send it to them. Follow up with phone calls or text messages if you don't get their feedback in 5 days.

THE SUPERHERO SURVEY

Superheroes know their superpowers. Do you? Sometimes our powers come so naturally to us that we don't even recognize them ourselves. So here's a fun survey to send to friends to get some 360-degree feedback and discover your superpowers and how they can be used professionally.

Warning: Side effects include increased happiness, greater self-awareness, & stronger friendships.

STEP 1. Cut, copy, paste, & edit the email template below.

Subject: Looking for some quick peer support...

Hey,

I hope all is well.

As you know, I'm always looking to grow and I value what you think about me. I found this fun survey for friends to give feedback to one another regarding their strengths, passions, and careers. I'm only sending it to 5 people and one of them is you!

Can you please take 5 minutes to complete the survey at the link below? It's only 6 questions. Your answers will help me tremendously as I consider what's next for me. The more specific your answers, the better.

http://www.careerchangechallenge.com/superherosurvey

I'll share with you what I discover about myself.

Sincerely,

STEP 2. Select 5 close friends to e-mail it to.

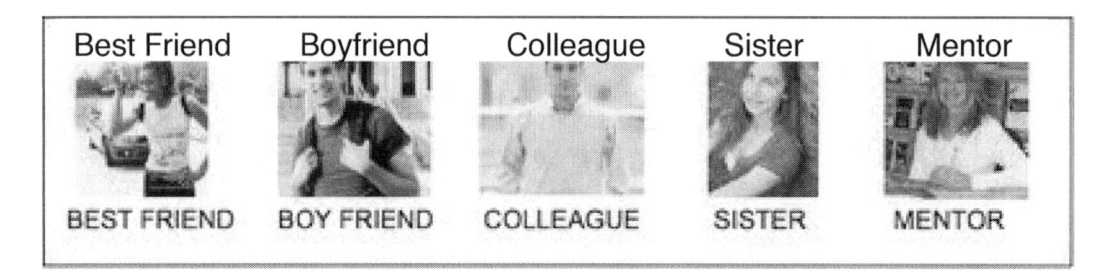

Best Friend	Boyfriend	Colleague	Sister	Mentor
BEST FRIEND	BOY FRIEND	COLLEAGUE	SISTER	MENTOR

Above are examples of the types of people you may want to send the email to. Make sure you choose 5 or more people you think will be honest with you and have demonstrated commitment to your success in the past.

They will take the survey and you will get this...

SUPERHERO SURVEY SAMPLE RESULTS

Your Name *	███████████
Your Email *	███████████
Name of the friend who sent this to you: *	███████████
The email address that they sent it from: *	███████████
1. POWERS: If you had to give your friend a nickname or superhero name, what would it be? And why?	La Paciente (The Patient One)-this is the first thing that came to mind. She shows great discipline and sticks through things even when they are hard.
2. PASSIONS: What activities would you say your friend is most passionate about doing? And why?	She is passionate about healthy living. I'm always impressed with your ability to stick to exercise routines and healthy eating. Great w/ budgets and coordination. You are also passionate about fashion and you are very stylish. You have a good eye for putting things together.
3. POTENTIAL PATHS: What potential professional paths could you see your friend being great at? And why?	Nutritionist, Stylist, Fashion Consultant, Own a business, Museum work, Women's Wellness
4. PERFORMANCE: When have you see your friend exhibit excellence? What impressed you about it?	I'm impressed by her ability to manage her lifestyle. she travels, manages her time well and is very independent. she can make decisions and move on. she's thoughtful and not impulsive which provides here with security.
5. RECOMMENDATIONS: Are there any companies, organizations, books, websites, or people you recommend they explore based on your suggestions above?	Def. the Alchemist Start Where You Are: A Guide to Compassionate Living by Pema Salvation: Black People and Love and All About Love by Bell Hooks Start Tapping the Power Within by Iyanla Vanzant Finding Soul on the Path of Orisa by Tobe Melora Correal Books by Thich Nhat Hanh TED videos r great. I can help identify people once I know which direction you're heading.
6. PEER SUPPORT: How do you hope to continue supporting your friend on the journey of life?	I don't have money but I can listen, share ideas, connect w/ people and u can come visit me. :)
6a. What resources are you willing to contribute specifically:	• My time • My network • LOVE • Advice/Ideas

DAY
09

2.2 HOW TO GET TESTIMONIALS FROM PEOPLE WHO KNOW YOU

Video Time: 7 minutes
Activity Time: 20 minutes

Required Tools:
- a LinkedIn account

Language:
None

Directions:
1. Identify 2-4 senior professionals that know who you are and can vouch for the quality of your work. See if they are LinkedIn.
2. Send the email template to 2-4 people. If you don't get a response via email, follow up with a call. If necessary, offer to write the testimonials for them.
3. Send thank you cards immediately after receiving the testimonials.

NAME	WHAT QUALITIES CAN THEY SPEAK TO ABOUT YOU?

EMAIL TEMPLATE

Hi Hal,

I hope all is well with you and your family.

Purpose: I'm writing to:
1. Ask you if it's okay to put you down as a reference on my resume.
2. Get a 3-5 sentence testimonial from you that speaks to who I am and the quality of my work.

Context: I've been doing some deep introspection lately and I'm positioning myself for a big change that will hopefully accelerate my career in corporate consulting. Below is my 30 Second Elevator Pitch and new career vision.

Usage: I will include your testimonial in the references section of my resume along with two others. If you have a LinkedIn account, it would help a lot if you recommended me there as well by simply copying and pasting what you wrote. Click here to go to my profile and then click on "Recommend this person."

Thank you in advance,

Jullien Gordon

....
My 30 Second Elevator Pitch

My name is Jullien Gordon and I'm a PurposeFinder. My work makes it possible for people who hate their jobs to address underemployment & underpay and experience what it means to make a living doing what you love. I have a Tony Robbins-like passion for helping people align their purpose, passions, and profession and I envision a world where everyone is making their highest contribution daily.

2.3 HOW TO CREATE PROFESSIONAL BUSINESS CARDS FOR CHEAP

Video Time: 6 minutes
Activity Time: 20 minutes

Required Tools:
- $10 for shipping

Language:
None

Directions:
1. Go to http://www.vistaprint.com (or http://www.moo.com).
2. At Vistaprint.com select "Free Products" > "Free Business Cards".
3. Model your card using the exact same template and fields shown.
4. Get 250 cards for free. Only pay shipping & handling ($5.67 for 21 day or $9.52 for 14 days).

Vistaprint — Make an impression.

NOW AVAILABLE : Email Marketing

| Home | Specials | Select a Country | En Español | Order Status | Help | | Log In | My Account | Cart |

Customize Your Free Business Card: Front side

Select from 45 designs!

① Enter text for front side

Company Name
JULLIEN GORDON

Full Name

Job Title
PurposeFinder

Address Line 1
bio, resume, & more at:

Address Line 2
www.julliengordon.com

Phone / Other   800# FREE Trial!
(646) 875-8477

Fax / Other

E-mail / Other
jullien@julliengordon.com

Web / Other   FREE Website!

[Add a Map]

Check My Spelling
Have the spell checker scan your document to check for typos

Exclusive Offers
Become a Vistaprint Insider to receive exclusive offers and tips.

Enter e-mail address
[Sign Up]

② Select your design

< 1 2 3 4 >

View premium Designs - only $19.99
Select Industry or Styles

▸ See hundreds of other designs - only $19.99!
▸ Use your photos and logos - only $24.98!

JULLIEN GORDON

PurposeFinder

JULLIEN@JULLIENGORDON.COM

BIO, RESUME, & MORE AT: (646) 875-8477
WWW.JULLIENGORDON.COM

[Remove Sample Text]

---

www.CareerChangeChallenge.com   Copyright © 2010 Jullien Gordon

2.4 HOW TO CREATE HEAD SHOTS AT HOME

Video Time: 3 minutes
Activity Time: 60 minutes

Required Tools:
- digital camera
- lights or sun
- a friend

Language:
None

Directions:
1. Find, clean, and iron a business outfit and a casual outfit and do your best to replicate these shots and angles.
2. Take your business photo inside with a plain wall or an office-like background.
3. Take your casual photo outside with a hint of nature in the background.

CASUAL PHOTOS

BUSINESS PHOTOS

DAY 10

2.5 HOW TO WRITE THE WORLD'S BEST RESUME EVER

Video Time: 6 minutes
Activity Time: 90 minutes

Required Tools:
- current resume
- job description
- red pen and/or highlighter

Language:
Point A to B Resume = a resume that uses a particular format for bulleting to express your maximum value

Directions:
1. Read the article below to understand why I teach resumes this way.
2. Print the ONE DAY RESUME packet http://ecourse.careerchangechallenge.com/wp-content/uploads/2010/08/Career-Change-Challenge-One-Day-Resume-Packet.pdf.
3. Go to http://ecourse.careerchangechallenge.com/upgrade/one-day-resume/, watch each video and complete each action item.

Dear Resume Writer,

Your resume should not be a carbon copy of your job description.

Most people simply find the job description that attracted them to the job they're transitioning from (and usually hate), copy and paste it into their resume and think they are done. WRONG! That's the surefire way of attracting more of what you did instead of more of what you want to do in the future. Most people's bullet points kill them.

BULLET POINTS THAT KILL

* Lead the sales team for our leading product and managed a team of 15 people
* Completed weekly product reports to evaluate performance and progress
* Supervised and trained 40 new staff members for the sales division
* Led weekly staff meetings focused on employee development

The #1 thing you want to communicate is that you CREATE VALUE.

A resume speaks to the patterns of behavior you will resume at your new jobs and the #1 thing to communicate is that you CREATE VALUE wherever you go. If you've worked at a place for more than a year and can't speak to how you created change in that organization, then I wouldn't hire you. The sad thing is that people do great things in their organizations, but for some reason they don't effectively communicate it on their resumes. Wherever your next job is—whether it's in the same industry or especially if it's in a new one—you need poignant points that communicate the value you created while you were there.

I call this the Point A to B (Point A2B) resume. The basic premise is, how did you move your last organization and/or yourself from Point A (where it was when you got there) to Point B (where it is when you leave). That's how value is created. You can read more on value creation in my post on increasing your personal velocity here. The bullets for the same resume as above using the Point A to B resume model would look as follows:

POIGNANT POINTS

* Built a sales team of 5 to 15 and increased the market share of our leading product by 10%
* Established an online accountability process to evaluate weekly progress that didn't exist before

* Created a sales training curriculum that increased retention rates and first year sales of 40 new employees

Bullet #1: Point A = team of 5 » Point B = team of 15
Bullet #1: Point A = market share of N% » Point B = market share of N+10%
Bullet #2: Point A = no accountability process » Point B = online accountability process
Bullet #3: Point A = N% retention rate » Point B = > N% retention rate
Bullet #3: Point A = $N first year sales » Point B = > $N first year sales

Conclusion

The best source of content for your resume is probably in your quarterly or yearly evaluations from your boss—not your job description. A lot of times it just means thinking deeper about what you did and rephrasing what you already have. If you didn't create any value at your last organization, then I don't know what to tell you. Why would a potential employer want someone who didn't create any value at their last job? I guarantee that the Point A to Point B resume will be more effective at getting you the job you desire than the traditional job description resume.

Jullien N. Gordon
443 Hancock Street #3, Brooklyn, NY 11233 · (310) 702-0891 · Jullien.gordon@gmail.com
www.julliengordon.com

Education

Stanford Graduate School of Business Stanford, CA
Masters of Business Administration & Education 9/2005-7/2007
- Leadership Development Platform, Fellow
- Black Business Student Association, Co-President
- Public Management Certificate

University of California, Los Angeles, June 2003 Los Angeles, CA
- Business Economics major with concentrations in Accounting and Education 8/2000-6/2003
- STOCKS & BONDS, Founder & President
- African Men's Collective, Chief of Staff & Annual Conference Organizer
- African Student Union Finance Coordinator and High School Conference Co-Chair

Experience

The Department of Motivated Vehicles New York, NY

Chief Executive Officer 8/2008-1/2009
- Published two books, *The 8 Cylinders of Success: How To Align Your Personal & Professional Purpose* and *Good Excuse Goals: How To End Procrastination & Perfectionism Forever*
- Created a powerful one-day curriculum for Driving School for Life to help millennials discover their purpose
- Addressed sizable audiences at Stanford, UCLA, Cornell, and the University of Michigan
- Issued 190 Licenses to Live to graduates of Driving School for Life in New York, San Francisco, Los Angeles, Washington DC, and New Orleans
- Inspire the lives of 1,000+ subscribers through weekly post on my blog, "Reminders to Myself"
- Hosted 23 consecutive monthly potlucks creating a safe space for 250+ young adults in the New York to support one another

Mylinia.com New York, NY

Chief Executive Officer 1/2006-1/2009
- Raised $75,000 in capital through angel investors and placing in the top 3 in two business plan competitions
- Built a team of 5 to strengthen the marketing, partnership, product design, and sales divisions of the business
- Negotiated a strong technology partnership to iterate on the technology until we are able to build an internal technology team

Management Leadership for Tomorrow New York, NY

Associate Director of Talent Recruitment 8/2008-1/2009
- Led and aligned a team of 3 on national marketing strategies for MLT's flagship programs, MBA Prep and Career Prep
- Successfully condensed the MBA Prep recruiting season from 7 months to 3.5 months, yielding 607 applications, up 25%
- Established fellow-driven ambassador programs to enhance regional presence and foster leadership development for fellows
- Developed processes around customer engagement to allow more data-driven decision making for future marketing tactics
- Designed and facilitated presentations on the MBA Value Proposition for 500+ young professionals nationwide

Talent Recruitment Manager 8/2007-8/2008
- Created a marketing strategy that increased Career Prep applications by 42% in one year, yielding 537 applications
- Managed MLT's web strategy which included a website redesign, SEO, and the introduction of various web 2.0 strategies
- Design curriculum and facilitated presentations for 300+ Career Prep fellows to aid their personal and professional growth

University of California Office of the President Oakland, CA

Consultant 6/2005-9/2005
- Developed a self-development curriculum and manual for the statewide Society of Learners
- Assessed the complete needs of the 15 charter members of the Connection Communities Coalition
- Planned as a member of the finance and communications sub-committees
- Developed a comprehensive marketing strategy to increase the universities eligible applicant pool
- Helped devise a 10-year plan to increase the number of UC-eligible African American students

S.H.A.P.E. Program Los Angeles, CA

Program Director 7/2003-6/2005
- Supervise 32 part-time staff members, 10 internal committees, and the academic success of over 150 Inglewood Unified School District school students grades six through twelve
- Wrote quarterly proposals, grants, and program evaluations
- Solidified and managed over $200,000 in funding over a two year period
- Revamped organizational structure to be more outcome oriented by creating 10 internal committees headed by staff members based on their personal strengths and interests
- Developed a comprehensive Microsoft Access database to improve student tracking, outcomes assessment, and program evaluation
- Negotiated a promising 4-way partnership with the Inglewood Unified School District, City of Inglewood Parks and Recreation Department, and the South Bay Workforce Investment Board
- Diversified the program's constituency to be more reflective of the demographics of Inglewood by hiring Chicano staff and administration, translating outreach materials, and adjusting our curriculum
- Designed and implemented a life skill building curriculum that allows students to apply their education through the use of creative and interactive activities and discussions based on school district standards

Robinsons May Department Stores North Hollywood, CA

Summer Intern 7/2002-9/2002
- Researched and generated innovative marketing strategies to bolster departmental sales (ex. Incorporating debuting kid's movies into company sales plan like the fast food industry)
- Assessed seasonal buying trends by store for young men's clothing and distributed orders accordingly
- Helped organize a company-wide summer young men's clothing departmental conference
- Corresponded with department supervisors, store managers, and vendors
- Helped prepare back-to-school advertising and store layouts

Leadership

- Founder & CEO of Mylinia.com, an online personal transformation platform and life management system
- Founder & CEO of G.I.F.T.E.D. (the Gordon Institute For Teaching & Educational Development)
- CFO of WoodWorks Records, LLC a R&B and hip hop label based in Inglewood, CA

Passions

- Personal development, Life coaching, Education, Writing, Soccer, Billiards, Reading, Entrepreneurship, Spirituality

Point A to B resume bullet example

VERB:	Pioneered
WHAT:	a Go Green Save Green recycling program
POINT A:	decreasing our waste
POINT B:	by half
ACTION:	by leveraging video conferencing for regional meetings

13 Cs of Killer Resume Bullets

1. Customer or Consumer: Write 1-2 bullet points about how you moved a metric related to customers from Point A to B (i.e. loyalty, satisfaction, dollars per purchase, net promoter score, etc.)

....

....

....

....

2. Cash Flow: Write 1-2 bullet points about how you moved a metric related to cash flow from Point A to B (i.e. increased inflow, decreased outflow, etc.)

....

....

....

....

3. Company: Write 1-2 bullet points about how you moved a metric related to the company from Point A to B (i.e. rankings in best places to work, # of new clients, labour standards, decrease % of defective products & returns, etc.)

....

....

....

....

4. Colleagues: Write 1-2 bullet points about how you moved a metric related to your colleagues from Point A to B (i.e. retention, onboarding time decrease, grew full-time-equivalents (FTE), # of mentorship relationships established, # of 360-degree feedback sessions completed, % participated in company retreat, increase in job security, etc.)

....

....

....

....

5. Community: Write 1-2 bullet points about how you moved a metric related to the community from Point A to B (i.e. # of hours volunteered, matching funds, mentorships, dollars of pro bono work, etc.)

....

....

....

....

6. Capital: Write 1-2 bullet points about how you moved a metric related to the capital from Point A to B (i.e. increase in assets, decrease in debt, mergers, acquisitions, division sold, financing raised, etc.)

....

....

....

7. Culture: Write 1-2 bullet points about how you moved a metric related to the company culture from Point A to B (i.e. employee satisfaction, # of innovative projects, employee safety rating, etc.)

....

....

....

....

8. Campaign: Write 1-2 bullet points about how you moved a metric related to an internal or external campaign from Point A to B (i.e. page views, conversion rate, media impressions, subscribers, etc.)

....

....

....

....

9. Champion of Change: Write 1-2 bullet points about how you moved a metric related to a change you led from Point A to B (i.e. carbon emissions decrease, switched software & executed national training, shifted market from computers to consulting, etc.)

....

....

....

....

10. Communication: Write 1-2 bullet points about how you moved a metric related to the company communication from Point A to B (i.e. integrated a CMS, established meeting process & protocol, created a Wiki to share intelligence, etc.)

....

....

....

....

11. Competition: Write 1-2 bullet points about how you moved a metric related to the competition from Point A to B (i.e. passed Toyota for #1 spot, increased market share by 10%, competition closed 5 stores in new market, etc.)

....

....

....

....

12. Collaboration: Write 1-2 bullet points about how you moved a metric related to collaboration or partnerships from Point A to B (i.e. built new supplier relationship, landed $100K sponsorship, led cross-divisional team to create new product, etc.)

....

....

....

....

13. Concepts: Write 1-2 bullet points about how you moved a metric related to concepts you created from Point A to B (i.e. created a new business line that grew to $4M, revamped lead generation process using my 4Ps framework, etc.)

....

....

....

....

SHAWN "JAY-Z" COREY CARTER

PROFILE
An entrepreneur and recording artist who has established and led corporations and products to new levels of international success in a variety of industries and cutting-edge markets. Proven ability to create and mold a brand image and successfully convey that vision to the masses, resulting in significant growth of enterprise value.

STRENGTHS AND ABILITIES
- Mass Media Communication
- Strategic Alliances & Joint Ventures
- Creative Concepts
- Impeccable Rhyme Skills
- New Project Development
- Product Introductions & Launches
- Branding & Expansion
- Market Analysis
- Business Opportunity Identification

PROFESSIONAL EXPERIENCE

LIVE NATION, Beverly Hills, Calif.   2008-Present
Contracted Artist
- Negotiated $150 million, 10-year recording, touring, and investments deal to create Roc Nation sub-division, which includes shares in Live Nation that will go to his Marcy Media company.

TRANSLATION ADVERTISING, New York, N.Y.   2008-Present
Co-Chairman
- Co-founded agency to help marketers reach multicultural consumers; an estimated market of $2 trillion per year.
- Provides clients with a range of marketing products, giving solid input on creative and entrepreneurial ideas.

J HOTELS, New York, N.Y.   2008-Present
Co-Owner
- Negotiated real estate deal, along with partners, to acquire a $66 million parcel of land in Manhattan.
- Overseeing the construction of the flagship location of an upscale hotel chain: 150,000-square-foot luxury property.

ROC APPAREL GROUP/SCION, LLC, New York, N.Y.   2008-Present
Founder
- Purchased brand management, licensing, and high-end fashion line with Iconix Brand Group, which now includes Artful Dodger.

The Spotted Pig, New York, N.Y.   2004-Present
Investor
- Invested in successful upscale "gastropub" with Michael Stipe and Mario Batali, among others.

NEW JERSEY NETS, East Rutherford, N.J.   2004-Present
Co-Owner
- Invested in NBA basketball team that will move to Brooklyn, N.Y., for 2010-2011 season.
- Acted as a representative of team at the 2008 NBA Draft Lottery.

40/40 CLUB, New York, N.Y.   2003-Present
Co-Founder/Co-Owner
- Launched upscale sports bar/lounge known for live music, celebrity patrons, and rare memorabilia.
- Built and managed successful outposts of the club in Atlantic City and Las Vegas, with more locations to follow.

ROCAWEAR, New York, N.Y.   1999-Present
Co-Founder/Chief Creative Officer
- Co-created company that redefines and redirects urban fashions and accessories to a mainstream audience.
- Amasses annual sales of more than $750 million since company launch, constantly expanding the line.
- Comandeered co-branding deals with various companies to increase market share.
- Sold company in 2007 to Iconix Apparel Group. Remains in charge of product development, marketing, and licensing.

ROC-A-FELLA RECORDS, New York, N.Y.   1996-2007
Co-Founder/Chief Creative Officer
- Co-founded record label, and began a flourishing recording career.
- Responsible for successfully seeking out and signing emerging talent to expand the label.
- Acquired and oversaw U.S. distribution rights for the Scottish, hand-crafted, triple-distilled vodka, Armadale.

DEF JAM RECORDINGS, New York, N.Y.   2004-2007
President
- Performed various duties as President and developed creative strategies to increase revenue.
- Signed and launched new and successful pop and contemporary R&B singers, such as Rihanna and Ne-Yo.

EDUCATION
George Westinghouse High School, Brooklyn, N.Y. *General Studies*
The Block, Marcy Projects, Brooklyn, N.Y. *The Game*

CO-PROMOTION DEALS & ENDORSEMENTS
COCA-COLA, *Cherry Coke*
REEBOK, *S. Carter Collection*
GENERAL MOTORS, created *"Jay-Z Blue"* color
ANHEUSER-BUSCH, *Budweiser Select*
HEWLETT-PACKARD, *Pavillion laptops*
- Collaborates on strategic marketing and creative ad development campaigns to reach a wider audience.

ACHIEVEMENTS & PHILANTHROPIC ENDEAVORS
- Led Forbes The Celebrity 100 list/Power Rank No. 7 2008.
- Selected as *British GQ's* International Man of the Year 2006.
- Participated in MSN's Strategic Account Summit.
- Starred in a Public Service Announcement with Russell Simmons on anti-Semitism.
- Invited to speak at United Nations and pledged to raise awareness regarding the world's water crisis.
- Along with Diddy, pledged $1 million to the American Red Cross' relief effort to aid victims of Hurricane Katrina.

REFERENCES

MEMPHIS BLEEK
Hip Hop Artist

STEVE STOUTE
Co-Chairman,
Translation Advertising

MICHAEL RAPINO
CEO, Live Nation

ANTONIO "L.A." REID
Chairman, Island/
Def Jam Music Group

---

www.CareerChangeChallenge.com   132   Copyright © 2010 Jullien Gordon

Metrics to Mention

Financial: Measures the economic impact of actions on growth, profitability and risk from shareholder's perspective (net income, ROI, ROA, cash flow).

Customer: Measures the ability of an organization to provide quality goods and services that meet customer expectations (customer retention, profitability, satisfaction and loyalty).

Internal Business Processes: Measures the internal business processes that create customer and shareholder satisfaction (project management, total quality management, Six Sigma).

Learning and Growth: Measures the organizational environment that fosters change, innovation, information sharing and growth (staff morale, training, knowledge sharing).

Productivity: Measures employee output (units/ transactions/dollars), the uptime levels and how employees use their time (sales-to-assets ratio, dollar revenue from new customers, sales pipeline).

Quality: Measures the ability to meet and/or exceed the requirements and expectations of the customer (customer complaints, percent returns, DPMO -- defects per million opportunities).

Profitability: Measures the overall effectiveness of the management organization in generating profits (profit contribution by segment/customer, margin spreads).

Timeliness: Measures the point in time (day/week/ month) when management and employee tasks are completed (on-time delivery, percent of late orders).

Process Efficiency: Measures how effectively the management organization incorporates quality control, Six Sigma and best practices to streamline operational processes (yield percentage, process uptime, capacity utilization).

Cycle Video Time: Activity Time: Measures the duration of time (hours/days/months) required by employees to complete tasks (processing time, time to service customer).

Resource Utilization: Measures how effectively the management organization leverages existing business resources such as assets, bricks and mortar, investments (sales per total assets, sales per channel, win rate).

Cost Savings: Measures how successfully the management organization achieves economies of scale and scope of work with its people, staff and practices to control operational and overhead costs (cost per unit, inventory turns, cost of goods).

Growth: Measures the ability of the management organization to maintain competitive economic position in the growth of the economy and industry (market share, customer acquisition/retention, account penetration).

Innovation: Measures the capability of the organization to develop new products, processes and services to penetrate new markets and customer segments (new patents, new product rollouts, R&D spend).

Technology: Measures how effectively the IT organization develops, implements and maintains information management infrastructure and applications (IT capital spending, CRM technologies implemented, Web-enabled access).

DAY

11

2.6 HOW TO THINK, TALK, & ACT LIKE YOU ALREADY WORK THERE

Video Time: 6 minutes
Activity Time: 60 minutes

Required Tools:
None

Language:
60 Second Business Plan = a quick analysis of an industry's or business' inputs, outputs, outcomes, and income cycle
Business Model = the way in which a company invest its resources, delivers products or services, creates customers, and earns a profit
Key Performance Indicators = the top metrics that are correlated to success in a given industry or company

Directions:
1. Complete the business model for your target industry to the best of your ability.
2. Complete the business model for your target company to the best of your ability.

2. OUTPUTS

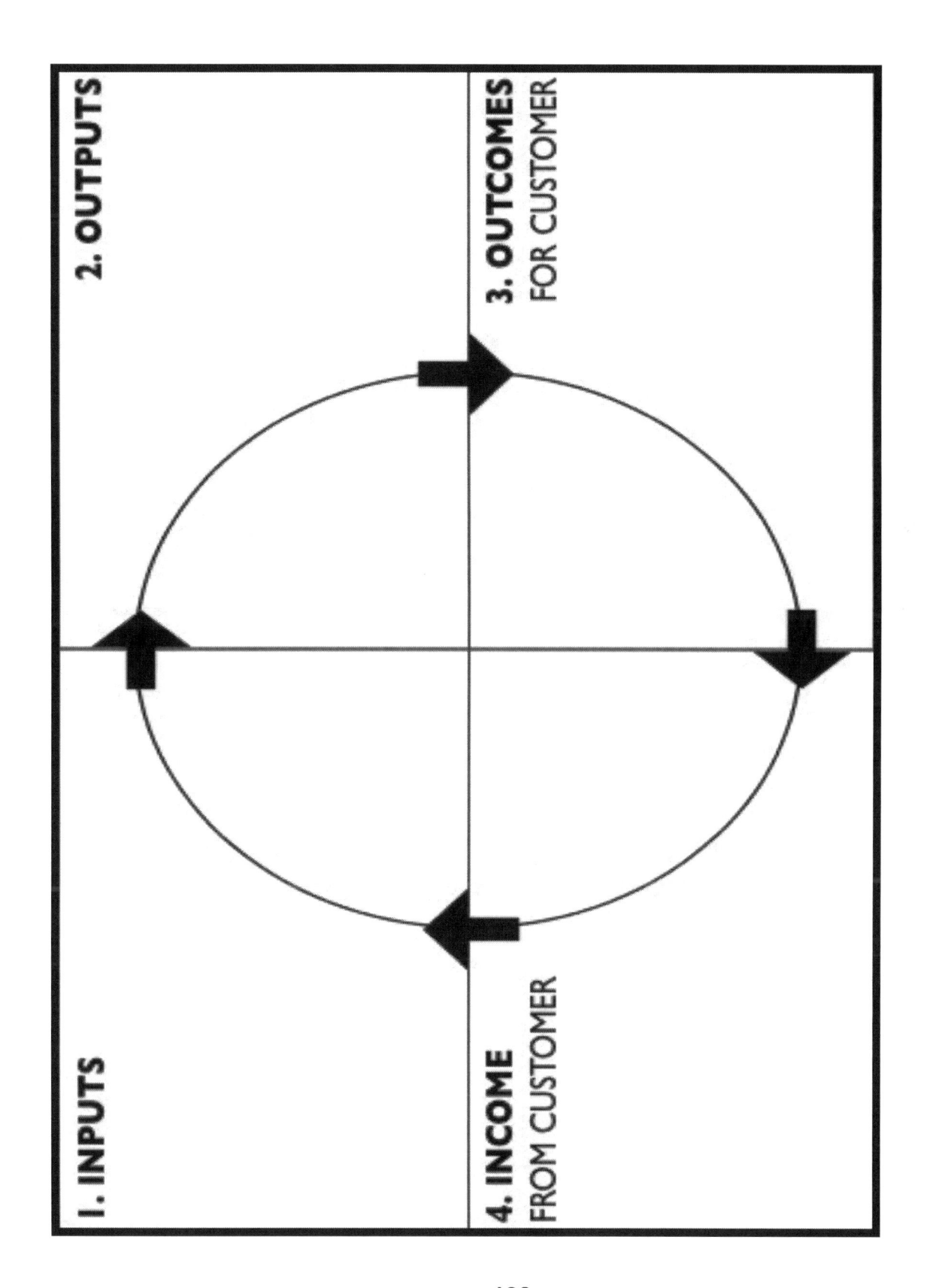

3. OUTCOMES
FOR CUSTOMER

1. INPUTS

4. INCOME
FROM CUSTOMER

2. OUTPUTS

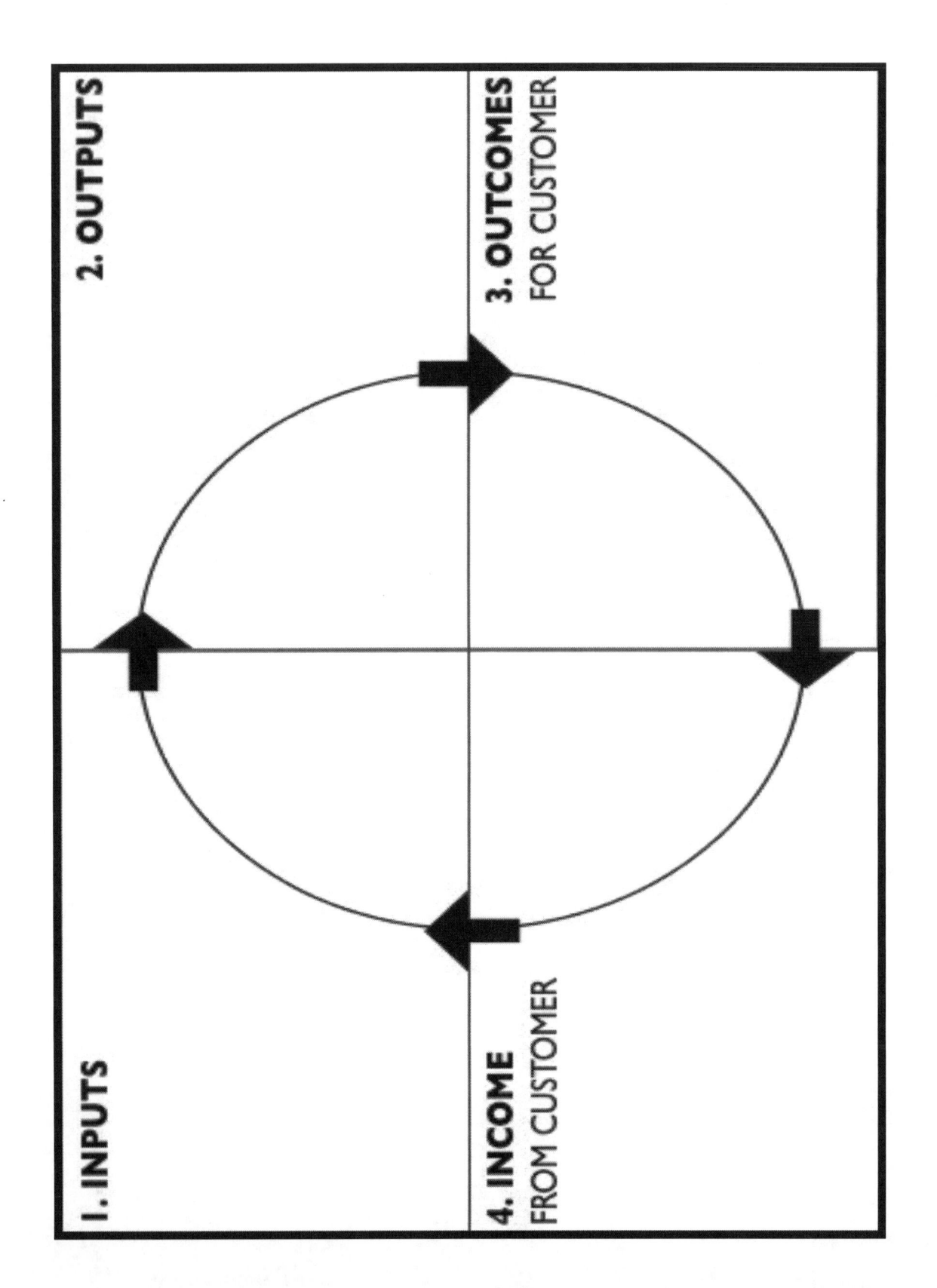

3. OUTCOMES FOR CUSTOMER

1. INPUTS

4. INCOME FROM CUSTOMER

	WHAT ARE THE KEY PERFORMANCE INDICATORS?
INPUTS - HUMAN RESOURCES - FINANCIAL RESOURCES - PHYSICAL RESOURCES	1
	2
	3
OUTPUTS - PRODUCTS - SERVICES	1
	2
	3
OUTCOMES - RESULTS FOR CUSTOMER	1
	2
	3
INCOME - CASH - BRAND - ETC.	

	HOW CAN YOU INCREASE/DECREASE THIS KPI?
INPUTS - HUMAN RESOURCES - FINANCIAL RESOURCES - PHYSICAL RESOURCES	1
	2
	3
OUTPUTS - PRODUCTS - SERVICES	1
	2
	3
OUTCOMES - RESULTS FOR CUSTOMER	1
	2
	3
INCOME - CASH - BRAND - ETC.	

2.7 HOW TO WRITE A GREAT COVER LETTER

Video Time: 4 minutes
Activity Time: 20 minutes

Required Tools:
- current cover letter

Language:
None

Directions:
1. Use the template below to create your cover letter.

COVER LETTER EXAMPLE

EMAIL SUBJECT: Dear Mr./Mrs. Hiring Manager, Referred by Mr. Big Shot

Jullien Gordon
1000 Hire Me Way
New York, NY 10001
jullien.gordon@gmail.com
(310) 353-2432

June 1, 2010

Employer Name
Address
City, State, Zip

Dear Mr./Mrs. Hiring Manager,

1st Paragraph

I am interested in learning more about the *Director of Recruitment* opening
(POSITION TITLE)

that *D. Smith, CEO of INC.* thought I would be a great fit for considering
(NAME & POSITION)

my *5* years of experience working *with the millennial generation*
(IN INDUSTRY, AS FUNCTION, OR WITH TARGET MARKET)

Currently I'm at *Opportunity Knocks* serving as their *Marketing Manager*
(YOUR COMPANY) (YOUR POSITION)

and I'm ready to advance my career and make more impact given my expertise.

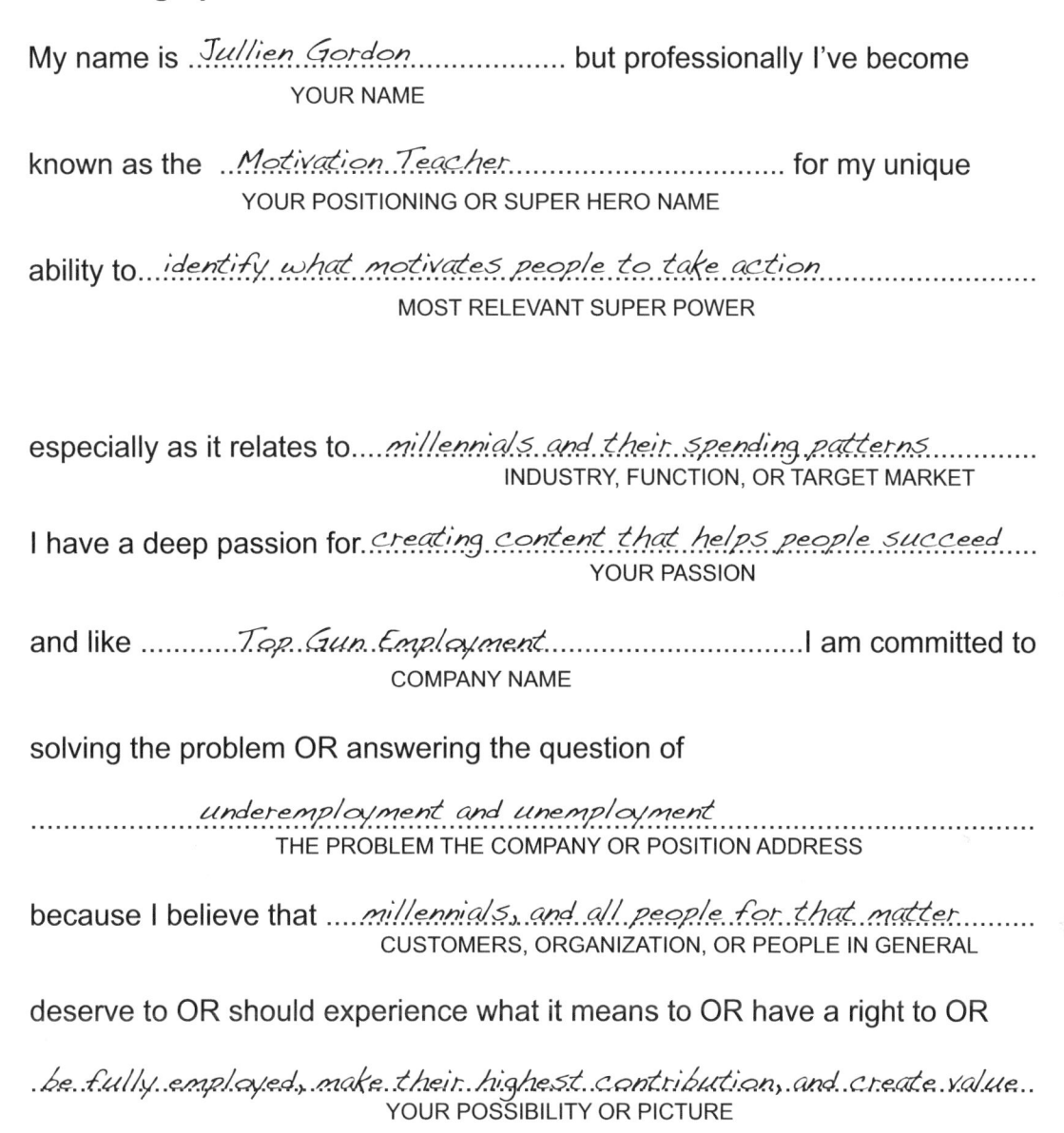

2nd Paragraph

My name is *Jullien Gordon* but professionally I've become
              YOUR NAME

known as the *Motivation Teacher* for my unique
             YOUR POSITIONING OR SUPER HERO NAME

ability to *identify what motivates people to take action*
             MOST RELEVANT SUPER POWER

especially as it relates to *millennials and their spending patterns*
             INDUSTRY, FUNCTION, OR TARGET MARKET

I have a deep passion for *creating content that helps people succeed*
             YOUR PASSION

and like *Top Gun Employment* I am committed to
             COMPANY NAME

solving the problem OR answering the question of

underemployment and unemployment
             THE PROBLEM THE COMPANY OR POSITION ADDRESS

because I believe that *millennials, and all people for that matter*
             CUSTOMERS, ORGANIZATION, OR PEOPLE IN GENERAL

deserve to OR should experience what it means to OR have a right to OR

be fully employed, make their highest contribution, and create value
             YOUR POSSIBILITY OR PICTURE

3rd Paragraph

I would love an invitation for a formal interview or an informational interview. Either way, I want to learn more about this position, the problem it is supposed to solve, and its success metrics as they relate to the company's strategy so that we can accurately assess my fit for the position together.

I have attached my résumé for your review. My résumé, portfolio, and bio can also be found at www.yourname.com if that's easier for you.

I welcome the chance to speak with you sometime and will follow up via phone if I don't hear from you in a week or so.

Sincerely,

Jullien Gordon
　　　YOUR NAME

DAY 12

2.8 HOW TO SET YOURSELF APART WITH A RESUME 2.0 OR PORTFOLIO

Video Time: 10 minutes
Activity Time: 90 minutes

Required Tools:
- Microsoft PowerPoint
- a Slideshare.net account
- samples of your professional work
- leather padfolio (optional)

Language:
None

Directions:
1. See Jullien's Resume 2.0 at http://julliengordon.mvmt.com/2009/11/26/allow-me-to-reintroduce-myself-jullien-gordons-resume-2-0/.
2. Use the slide templates provided by Jullien to create your resume 2.0.
3. Create a SlideShare.net account.
4. Upload your resume 2.0.
5. Get the embed code & add it to your website.

THE INTRO

SLIDE 1 TITLE: NAME & PROFESSIONAL PICTURE
SLIDE 2 TITLE: TABLE OF CONTENTS & INTENTION
SLIDE 3 TITLE: 30 SECOND PITCH

THE PAST

SLIDE 4 TITLE: LIFELONG LEARNER (=FORMAL & INFORMAL EDUCATION)
SLIDE 5 TITLE: LIFELONG LEADER
SLIDE 6 TITLE: PERSONAL ASSETS (=PASSIONS, SKILLS, & STRENGTHS)
SLIDE 7 TITLE: #1 ASSET WITH MULTIPLE EXAMPLES
SLIDE 8 TITLE: COMPANY #1 & VALUE CREATED THERE
SLIDE 9 TITLE: COMPANY #2 & VALUE CREATED THERE

THE PRESENT

SLIDE 10 TITLE: 8 CYLINDERS OF SUCCESS
SLIDE 11 TITLE: _____ (ROLE #2 & #3 IE FAMILY MAN, SOCCER COACH)
SLIDE 12 TITLE: PAST OR PRESENT PROJECTS
SLIDE 13 TITLE: DASHBOARD FOR SUCCESS
SLIDE 14 TITLE: SUCCESS SYSTEMS & ORGANIZATIONAL AFFILIATIONS (E.G. 30 DAY DO IT GROUP, MASTERMIND GROUP, CHURCH, MENTORS, PROFESSIONAL ORGS, TRAININGS)

THE FUTURE

SLIDE 15 TITLE: THREE PERSONAL & PROFESSIONAL GOALS
SLIDE 16 TITLE: VISION (=VISION BOARD, EULOGY, OR RETIREMENT SPEECH)
SLIDE 17 TITLE: CONTACT INFORMATION

ADDENDUM ITEMS (Convert Word documents to PDFs using http://www.freepdfconvert.com/)

- Business Plan
- Academic Work
- Professional Project
- Volunteer Project
- Extracurricular Activity
- Writing Sample (Article, Blog Post, Speech)
- PowerPoint
- Pictures
- Flyers
- Products
- Screenshots

DAY 13

2.9 HOW TO BUY WWW.YOURNAME.COM AND GET FIRSTNAME@YOURNAME.COM

Video Time: 13 minutes
Activity Time: 30 minutes

Required Tools:
- $11 for domain name

Language:
None

Directions:
1. Go to http://www.godaddy.com.
2. Try these different combinations.

Examples:
www.julliengordon.com (IDEAL)
www.julliengordon.org (.org instead of .com)
www.julliengordon.net (.net instead of .com)
www.julliengordon.me (.me instead of .com)
www.julliengordon.info (.info instead of .com)
www.jullienngordon.com (middle initial)
www.jullien-gordon.com (add hyphen)
www.jgordon.com (first initial only)
www.jngordon.com (first and middle initial)
www.thejulliengordon.com (add the to the front)
www.julliengordoninc.com (add inc to the end)

3. Enter this discount code "cjc749chp"
4. Purchase your domain name

EMAIL FORWARDING

1. Log in to your Account Manager.

2. In the My Products section, click Email.

3. Next to the account you want to use, click Manage Account.

4. If you have unused email plans, and have not previously disabled the pop-in message that displays, click View All to view your complete list of email plans.

5. On the left, click Forwarding Plans to use a forwarding plan you have already set up, or click Unused Forwarding, under the Unused Plans folder to use a new plan.

6. Click Add next to the Email Forwarding account you want to use.

7. Click Add for the forwarding account to which you want to add a forwarding address.

8. In the Add Forward field, enter the first part of the email address, i.e. the user name.

9. In the Forward Mail To field, enter the email address that you want to forward messages to.

10. To make the mailbox a catch-all account, select Yes. A catch-all account receives all messages sent to non-existent email addresses at your domain. For example, unknown@mydomain.com.

11. To set an automatic response for this account, select Auto-Responder, and then type the message in the Auto-responder message text box. You can also specify a date and time for the auto response to start and end. An auto-response allows you to automatically send a reply message to people who send you email messages.

12. Click OK.

DAY 14

2.10 HOW TO CREATE A FREE WEBSITE THAT WOOS POTENTIAL EMPLOYERS

Video Time: 34 minutes
Activity Time: 120 minutes

Required Tools:
- An account at http://www.weebly.com
- An account at http://docs.google.com
- Your updated resume 1.0
- A headshot of just yourself
- A YouTube.com video for Slideshare.net PowerPoint
- Your 3 blog entries on the problems you see, insights you have, and your passion for the industry you want to be employed in
- The Career Change Challenge Build Your Website PDF below the video

Language:
None

Great Examples:
http://www.julliengordon.weebly.com
http://socialjenny.com/
http://tomwantsajob.wordpress.com
http://www.michaelboezi.com

Go to http://www.weebly.com

Choose a site name

Choose option C, "I already have my own domain name"

Copy the Follow the instructions to change the A record

Copy the 11-digit number they give you and then go to www.godaddy.com and log in.

1. First login to GoDaddy.

2. On the main menu, click on the "Domain Manager" link in the toolbar on the left side of the screen.

3. Click on the domain name you are configuring.

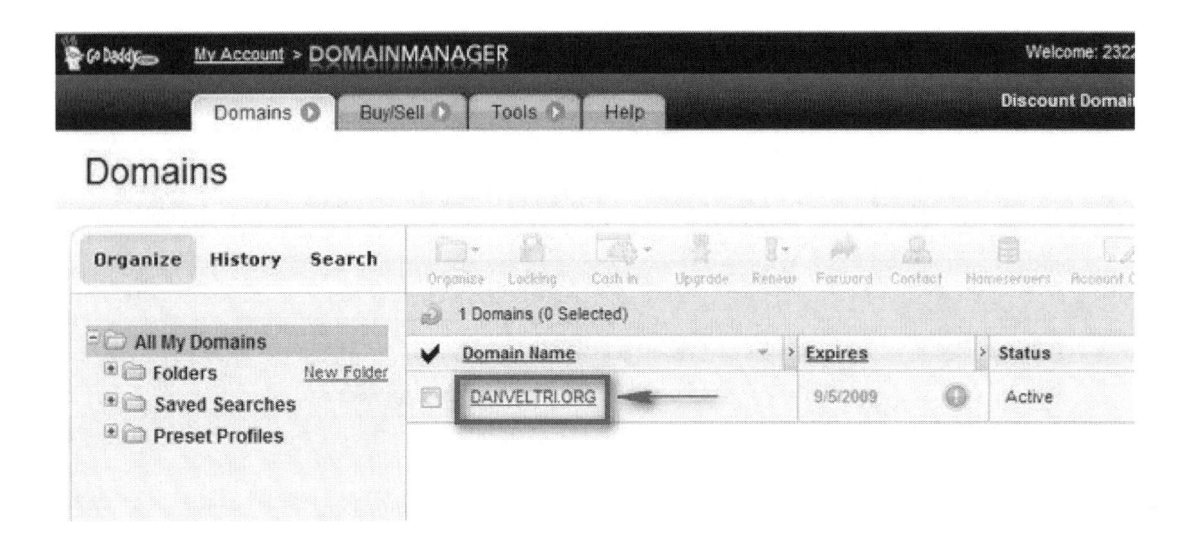

4. Click on the "Total DNS Control" link.

Note: If, under "Total DNS" you see a message that says "DNS not hosted here", proceed to these instructions.

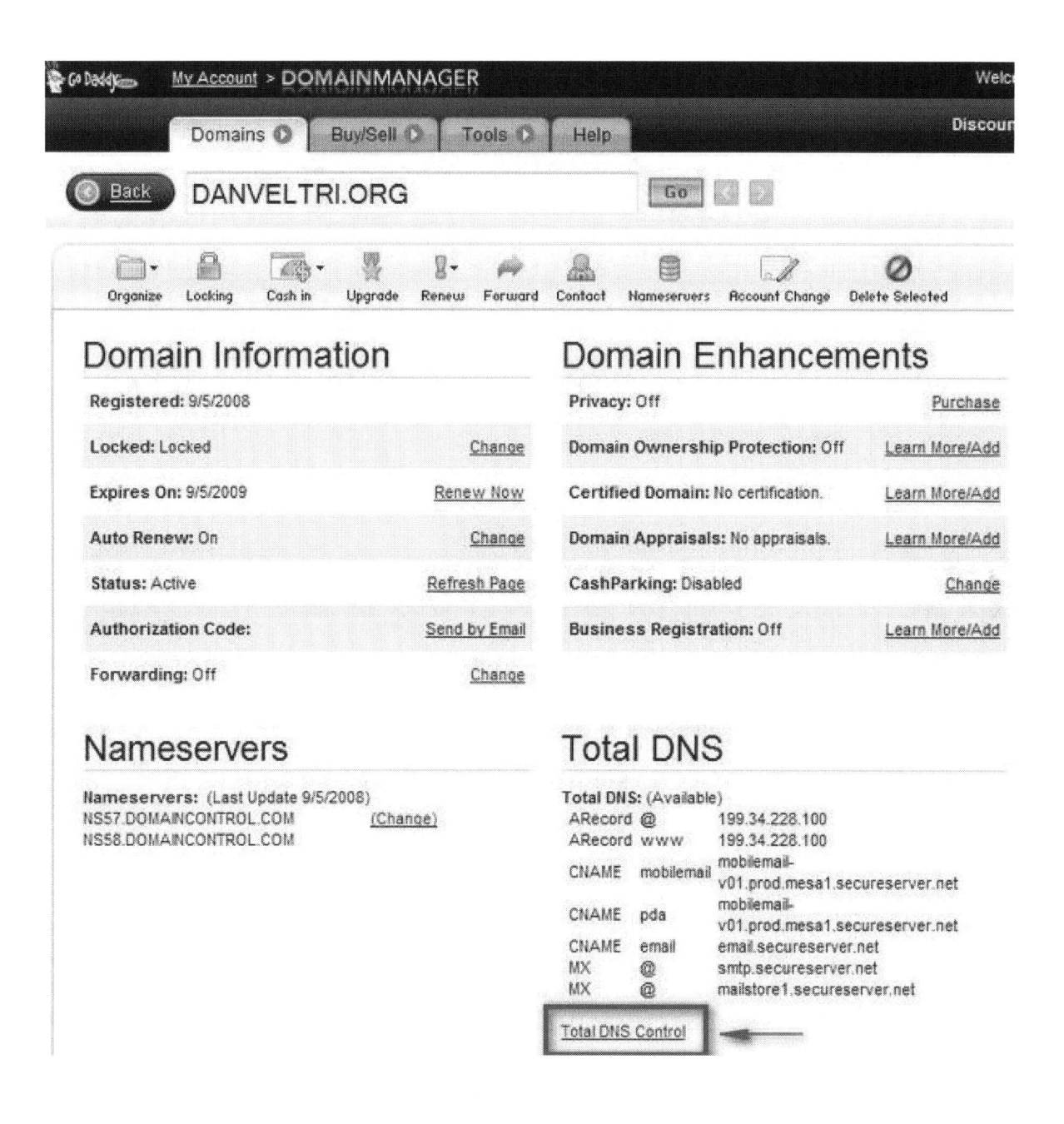

5. Delete all existing A-Records and the CNAME with host "www".

6. Setup two new A-Records as follows:

- For the first A-Record, set the host to "@" and the points to IP address to "199.34.228.100"
- For the second A-Record, set the host to "www" and the points to IP address to "199.34.228.100"

Note: It can take up to 24-48 hours (although usually less) for these changes to take effect.

Check to see that your domain is correctly configured by <u>clicking here</u>.

You'll know your domain is ready once it directs you to a <u>Weebly branded 404 page</u>.

Once this occurs, just login to edit your Weebly site, click into the "settings" tab, "choose site address", and input "www.yourdomain.com" into Option C. If by chance, it says there is a problem, press continue anyway and republish the site.

For additional support look at: http://support.weebly.com/support/index.php?pg=kb.page&id=4 or call GoDaddy.com Support at (48) 505-8877.

Choosing a Design

Now go back to www.weebly.com and click the design button in the header and choose any theme with some sort of header image

Adding Content to your Homepage

Click on the header image and upload your professional photo

If you would like the resize your header image to fit the entire box, click the header image to get the header image size and then go to http://www.resize.it. Click "Advanced Tools". Upload the image. Enter the pixels from the header. Hit "Okay". Move the crop to where you want it. Hit "Crop It". Right click the image and "Save as..." "My Website Header".

Click "Elements" in the header

Drag "Two Column Layout" under your header image.

In the box on the left, drag "Paragraph with Text"

Add the title "My 30 Second Pitch" and then paste your 30 second pitch here.

In the box on the right, drag "Custom HTML"

In the code, change the 425px to 330px.

Embedding Multimedia

Get the embed code from Slideshare.net for your Resume 2.0. Change width="425" height="355" to width="330" height="270" twice within the code.

Drag another "Two Column Layout" under your original one.

In the box on the left, drag "Paragraph with Text"

Add the title "More About Me" and add a short bio that speaks to where you're from, your education, your personality, the various roles you play and hats you wear, and how you spend your free time.

Adding an RSS Feed

In the box on the right, add an RSS Feed Reader by selecting "More" in the "Elements" tab and dragging "Feed Reader" into the box

Click the box and for the "Feed Address" type in http://julliengordon.weebly.com/1/feed, except replace my name with your name.

Creating New Pages

Click the "Pages" tab

Click the "New Page" button and title it "Resume 1.0"

Click the "New Page" button and title it "Resume 2.0"

Click the "New Blog" button and title it "Blog"

Click the "New Page" button and title it "Downloads"

Click the "New Page" button and title it "Contact"

Click the "Save" button

Integrating Your Resume 1.0

Click on the "Resume 1.0" page

Drag "Custom HTML" under the header

Click on the box and click "Edit Custom HTML"

Paste this code in the box:

Go to <object data="http://docs.google.com/View?id=dc55sw65_970dm3pnzhd" width="700" height="2000"> <embed src="http://docs.google.com/View?

id=dc55sw65_970dm3pnzhd" width="700" height="2000"> Error: Embedded data could not be displayed. </object>

Go to Google Docs (http://docs.google.com) and open up your resume.

Click "File" and click "Make a copy"

Rename the document to "Resume for Web".

Remove your mailing address (and phone number if you want) from the heading.

In the right hand corner click "Share" and select "Publish as a webpage"

Click "Publish document"

Copy the URL that appears after you click the button.

Check the "Automatically re-publish" box

Go back to weebly.com and replace http://docs.google.com/View?id=dc55sw65_970dm3pnzhd with your new URL in two places in the code.

Adjust the height from 2000 (in two places) to fit your resume.

Integrating Your Resume 2.0

Click on the "Resume 2.0" page

Drag "Custom HTML" under the header

Click on the box and click "Edit Custom HTML"

Get the embed code from Slideshare.net for your Resume 2.0. Change width="425" height="355" to width="700" height="585" twice within the code.

Uploading Downloads

Click on the "Downloads" page

Click "More" which comes after "Multimedia" & "Revenue" in the "Elements" tab

Drag "File" down two times.

In the first file, upload your Resume 1.0

In the second file, upload your Resume 2.0

Feel free to add more files that demonstrate the quality of your work.

Adding Blog Entries

Click on the "Blog" page just to see how it looks. We're going to come back to that later.

Adding your Contact Information

Click on the "Contact" page

Drag "Paragraph with Title" under the header

Title it "Feel free to say hello"

Paste the text below:

Email: jullien@juliengordon.com
Phone: 646-875-8342
LinkedIn: http://www.linkedin.com/in/jullien
Facebook: http://www.facebook.com/jullien
Twittter: http://www.twitter.com/PurposeFinder

Substitute your contact information and links.

DAY
15

2.11 HOW TO USE 3 SIMPLE & SHORT BLOGS TO SHOW YOU ARE COMPETENT

Video Time: 8 minutes
Activity Time: 60 minutes

Required Tools:
- weebly.com

Language:
None

Directions:
1. Follow the directions below and complete the templates. You can type directly into your weebly.com blog at http://www.weebly.com/weebly/main.php instead of writing in the templates.
2. Publish the three new posts to your blog.

PASSION BLOG: 5 THINGS YOU MUST SEE IF YOU LIKE [PASSION HERE]

Key Questions:
- Why are you so passionate about this industry?
- When was the first time you realized this was your passion?
- What was your first influence? A book? A conference? A person? A website? An article? A television show? A movie?
- How are you actively engaging your passion today?
- What are 5 things you would recommend people who share your passion check out?

Entry Template

My passion for .... began in ....
                  Passion or Industry   Time, Year, Age, Grade

when I...
                                    Key Experience

From there it grew. I started ....
                            New Actions (Groups, Books, Subscriptions, Practice, etc)

....

Today my passion is like never before. I continue to ....
                                                             Forms of Practice

....

in addition to ....

I started this blog to start a conversation, learn from, and connect with those who share my passion. The top 3 resources that have supported me on my journey include:

1. ....

2. ....

3. ....

Please share any resources that have helped influence your passion by commenting below. Until next time...

PROBLEM BLOG: THE BIGGEST PROBLEM FOR [YOUR INDUSTRY] TODAY

Key Questions:
- What is the biggest problem in your industry today?
- What are your ideas on how it can be solved?
- What new innovations do you see potentially solving this problem? Which ones won't be effective and why?

Entry Template

The .... is evolving quickly as is the rest of the world.
              Industry

I remember when...
              Memory About The Industry 5-10 Years Ago

Since then, there have been three major trends that I've observed and I think we need to take into consideration because they will likely change the industry forever.

1. ....

....

2. ....

....

3. ....

....

The convergence of these three trends could result in......................................

....

....

Thus a great threat and opportunity—depending on how you look at it—is upon us. If you have any interesting thoughts, statistics, or opinions, feel free to leave them in the comments section below.

Thanks in advance,

INDUSTRY NEWS BLOG: RESPONSE TO [AUTHOR]'S IDEAS ON [SUBJECT]

Key Questions:
- What recent trends do you see in your industry? Who is impacted most by them? How do the trends affect decision making?
- If you could envision your industry 10 years from now, what would it look like?
- What are some of your assumptions about the future of your industry?

Entry Template

I recently read .... article (book or blog) titled
                                      Author

....
                                      Title

His/her main point can be captured in the quote, "..

....

...."

I totally dis/agree and here's why:

First and foremost, ...

....

On top of that,..

....

Finally, ...

....

In my opinion, our industry undervalues (or overvalues)..............................

....

And until we put the appropriate value on..
                                                    Subject of Debate

we won't realize our true potential to ....
                                                    Purpose of Industry

2.12 HOW TO EDIT ALL OF YOUR COPY FOR CONSISTENCY & GRAMMAR

Video Time: 2 minutes
Activity Time: 25 minutes

Required Tools:
- 3 copies of each your D.R.E.A.M. Catchers (resume 1.0, cover letter, resume 2.0, business cards, website homepage, and 3 blog entires)
- 3 folders
- 3 friends
- a printer

Language:
None

Directions:
1. Print three copies of your resume 1.0.
2. Print three copies of your resume 2.0.
3. Print three copies of your 3 blog entries.
4. Print three copies of your website homepage.
5. Make three packets with each document listed above inside.
6. Give the packets to three people who you know are perfectionists, neat freaks, or sticklers for grammar.
7. Edit all spelling errors and areas of confusion.
8. Address every grey box that has a check mark in it.

Career Changer's Name..

Editor's Name..

Due Date:................................. **Phone Number:**..

Thank you for agreeing to edit and audit my personal brand. The purpose of this activity is to develop my personal and professional brand and ensure quality and consistency.

Steps for each document
1. Please read each document out loud to yourself
2. Circle all spelling errors and areas of confusion
3. Mark YES or NO for each question below in the boxes below

Business Card

Y	N	
		Are there any spelling errors? Please circle them.
		Are there any confusing uses of language? Please circle them.
		Does the superhero name intrigue you and make you want to know more?
		Does the contact information match the information on the resume?

Additional Thoughts/Feedback/Comments:

....

....

....

....

....

....

Resume 1.0

Y	N	
		Are there any spelling errors? Please circle them.
		Are there any confusing uses of language? Please circle them.
		Does each bullet point communicate how the career changer moved something (a number, initiative, etc.) from some point A to some point B
		Are there any gaps in the dates on the resume?
		Does the name and contact information on the resume match what you see on the business cards?
		Do the resume bullet points look like a job description or a list of daily duties and responsibilities?

Additional Thoughts/Feedback/Comments:

....

....

....

....

....

....

....

....

....

....

Resume 2.0

Y	N	
		Are there any spelling errors? Please circle them.
		Are there any confusing uses of language? Please circle them.
		Is the layout clean and clear?
		Does each slide have a clear title and purpose?
		Do the images complement the text?

Additional Thoughts/Feedback/Comments:

....

....

....

....

....

....

....

....

Three Blog Entries

Y	N	
		Are there any spelling errors? Please circle them.
		Are there any confusing uses of language? Please circle them.
		Does the blog entry about a PROBLEM convey that the career changer has deep INSIGHTS about the industry?
		Does the blog entry about a PASSION convey that the career changer has deep COMMITMENT to the industry?
		Does the blog entry about the INDUSTRY convey that the career changer has clear VISION about the industry?
		Does the blog entry about the PUBLICATION convey that the career changer has INNOVATIVE THOUGHTS about the industry?

Additional Thoughts/Feedback/Comments:

....

....

....

....

....

....

....

....

....

....

Website Homepage

Y	N	
		Are there any spelling errors? Please circle them.
		Are there any confusing uses of language? Please circle them.
		Does the career changer's 30 second pitch capture you?
		Does the picture in the header look professional?
		Does the "More About Me" section give you insight into the career changer's personality and life outside of work?
		Is the "slideshow" displaying properly and working?
		Does the "download resume" link work?

Additional Thoughts/Feedback/Comments:

....

....

....

....

....

....

....

IMMEDIATELY RETURN THESE FORMS BACK TO THE PERSON WHO GAVE THEM TO YOU.

DAY

16

2.13 HOW TO MAXIMIZE YOUR LINKEDIN PROFILE & EXPAND YOUR NETWORKS

Video Time: 9 minutes
Activity Time: 30 minutes

Required Tools:
- a LinkedIn.com account
- a Facebook account

Language:
None

Directions:
1. Register and/or login to www.linkedin.com and check off every action item listed below.

LINKEDIN

EDITING YOUR LINKEDIN PROFILE

Overall
[] Complete the profile as thoroughly as possible

Basic Info
[] When editing your profile, put your superhero name for your "Professional Headline"
[] Upload your professional photo

Current & Past Employment
[] Add your last 3 most significant positions and copy and paste the bullet-points from your resume into the description
[] If the company is not a Fortune 500 company, add 1-2 sentences about it at the top of your description
[] If you've been promoted within the same organization, add those positions separately (to show your growth)

Recommendations
[] Request recommendations for specific positions (ideally 1 to 2 per position). Don't ask randomly. Call the person first. Tell them an email from LinkedIn is coming and offer to recommend them back.

Additional Information
[] For websites put www.YOURNAME.com as your website and add www.YOURNAME.com/blog as your blog
[] Add all of your passions to the interest section
[] Add all of your organizational affiliations (i.e. young professional group, church, fraternity, sorority, etc.)

Personal Information
[] Only add your phone number (preferably a Google Voice number that forwards to your real cell phone)

Public Profile
[] Edit it to be www.linkedin.com/in/YOURNAME

Applications
[] Link your resume 2.0 from Slideshare.net

EXPANDING YOUR LINKEDIN.COM NETWORK

ADDING CONTACTS

Import from Email
1. Go to https://www.linkedin.com/secure/importAndInvite?trk=tab_cn
2. Enter the email address you want to import contacts from
3. Enter your password
4. Only select the people with the [IN] symbol next to their name. It may take awhile to go through everyone, but it will help your research later.

Import Colleagues
1. Go to http://www.linkedin.com/reconnect?displayCategories=&trk=tab_cols
2. Only select the names of colleagues that you have worked on projects with or at least had lunch with

Import Classmates
1. Go to http://www.linkedin.com/edurec?display=&trk=tab_clas
2. Only select classmates who you would run after to talk to in an airport

People You May Know
1. Go to http://www.linkedin.com/pymk-results?full=
2. Only select people who you actually know

Groups
1. Go to http://www.linkedin.com/home?myGroups=&trk=hb_side_grps
2. Find any groups or organizations that you may be affiliated with (e.g. schools, fraternities, sororities, programs, etc.)

Evaluating Your Social Capital
1. Go to http://www.linkedin.com/connections?trk=hb_tab_cnts
2. Click the "colleagues" tag to see current and old colleagues
3. Click the "classmates" tag to see current and old classmates
4. Click "Companies" and you will see the top 10 companies that you have the most contacts at.
5. Click "Location" and you will see the top 10 cities/regions that you have the most contacts in.
6. Click "Industries" and you will see the top 10 industries that you have the most contacts in.
7. For 4, 5, & 6, to send a message, select all or select the individuals in the second column, and then click "Send Message" in the third column.

2.14 HOW TO MAXIMIZE YOUR FACEBOOK PROFILE & EXPAND YOUR NETWORKS

Video Time: 6 minutes
Activity Time: 15 minutes

Required Tools:
None

Language:
None

Directions:
1. Register and/or login to www.facebook.com and complete all of the action items below.

FACEBOOK

EDITING YOUR FACEBOOK PROFILE

Overall
[] Complete the profile with the eye of an HR representative without losing who you are

About Me
1. Condense your 30-second pitch to 15 seconds and paste it in the area under your profile picture
2. In the "Bio" section of your profile, either put www.YOURNAME.com or copy the "More About Me" section from www.YOURNAME.com
3. In the "Favorite Quotations" section, add a quote from someone you respect in your industry. For instance, I might put something like:

   "A real decision is measured by the fact that you've taken a new action. If there's no action, you haven't truly decided." - Tony Robbins

Photos
1. Roll over your profile photo in the upper right hand corner, click "Change picture," and upload your professional picture
2. Upload other professional profile pictures to balance out your personal ones
3. Click on your profile photo and save the ones to your desktop that you want to keep and then delete any "crazy" pictures
4. Skim through all of your photos to make sure there aren't any compromising photos there. Make sure to skim the photos you were tagged in and untag yourself if necessary.

Work & Education
1. Replicate what you did on LinkedIn
2. Add your "concentrations." It will help you with search later.

Books
1. Add some of the books you've read related to the industry to your favorite books list

Contact Information
1. Add your FIRSTNAME@YOURNAME.com to your email address
2. Add your Google Voice number to your profile
3. Add www.YOURNAME.com as your websites

Importing Your Blog
1. Go to http://www.facebook.com/help/?page=818#!/editnotes.php?import
2. Enter www.julliengordon.weebly.com/1/feed/

Getting Your Custom URL
1. Go to http://www.facebook.com/username/
2. Change your Facebook profile address to www.facebook.com/YOURNAME (i.e. www.facebook.com/jullien or www.facebook.com/julliengordon)

EXPANDING YOUR FACEBOOK NETWORK

ADDING CONTACTS

Import from Email
1. Go to http://www.facebook.com/home.php#!/find-friends/?ref=sb
2. Enter the email address you want to import contacts from
3. Enter your password
4. You will be befriended to everyone you select

Suggested Friends
1. Go to http://www.facebook.com/#!/find-friends/?expand=pymk&ref=hpb
2. Click "Add as friend" on people you recognize

MODULE THREE

Build Your D.R.E.A.M. Team

DAY 17

3.1 HOW TO BUILD YOUR SOCIAL CAPITAL IN 30 DAYS

Video Time: 6 minutes
Activity Time: 90 minutes

Required Tools:
- personal contacts

Language:
Social Capital = who you know and who knows you
Social Network = one's ability to get others to move on their behalf to get others to move on their behalf to achieve a particular outcome

Directions:
1. Create a list of 30 people and places in your social network.
2. Email, call, or text each one of them using the script provided.
3. As you schedule coffees, lunches, dinners, calls, and find events to go to, add them to the charts on the following pages.

TARGET 30

30 DAY DO IT GROUP: Friends who came to your first 30 Day Do It group meeting

1. ....
2. ....
3. ....
4. ....
5. ....
6. ....

NETWORK UP: Mentors, Professors, Family, Family Friends, & Old Bosses

7. ....
8. ....
9. ....
10. ....
11. ....
12. ....

NETWORK ACROSS: Friends, Old Classmates, Neighbors, Alumni events

13. ....
14. ....
15. ....
16. ....
17. ....
18. ....

NETWORK OUT: Client's companies, Organizations that helped you, Associations you're a member of, Honors Societies, Organizations you've volunteered for

19. ....
20. ....
21. ....
22. ....
23. ....
24. ....

NETWORK AROUND: Meetup.com, Networking events, Strangers, Everywhere (e.g. the subway, the coffee shop, the gas station, the grocery store)

25. ....
26. ....
27. ....
28. ....
29. ....
30. ....

NAME/EVENT	DATE & TIME	LOCATION
NYC Young Professionals Meetup	7/7 @ 6pm	AREA 51 in Manhattan

RESULTS	FOLLOW UP EMAILS
met 10 people, got 3 new job leads, invited to another event	sent

NAME/EVENT	DATE & TIME	LOCATION
Mark Addington of ACME INC	7/7 @ 12pm	Starbucks at 51st & 4th

RESULTS	FOLLOW UP EMAILS
passing my resume on internally & to friends in the industry	sent

Email Template

Hi ....,

I hope that you are well.

It's always good seeing you at ....
Event, Place, Organization

I admire your ....
Affirmation

and that's exactly the reason I'm reaching out to you.

I'm in the process of a career change and I need some of your....................................
Skill You Affirmed

I'm currently ....
Current Company & Position

But I would like to transition into ....
D.R.E.A.M. Job or Industry

Considering my passion for ....
Passion, Skill, and/or Subject

I was hoping I could have 15 minutes of your time for a call, quick coffee, or even lunch. Whatever works best for you.

You seem to love your work and that inspires me. I just want to know if you know of any opportunities that may fit me, have any contacts in the industry, or have general strategies that may help me along my career path.

I've attached my resume, but you can also view it online at ....
www.yourname.com

Let me know if you have the time.

Thanks in advance,

Your Name Here

DAY

18

3.2 HOW TO LEAVE WITH REAL RELATIONSHIPS, NOT JUST BUSINESS CARDS

Video Time: 6 minutes
Activity Time: 30 minutes

Required Tools:
None

Language:
None

Directions:
1. Determine how you want people to speak and feel about you after the event.
2. Based on that, write parking lot affirmation about who you're going to be at the event.
3. Considering who you're being, write down the types of things that person would do.
4. Write your parking lot affirmation on the back of one of your business cards and keep it with you at all times. Read it before entering any networking space.

1. HOW DO YOU WANT PEOPLE TO SPEAK ABOUT YOU AFTER THAT SPACE?

I recently met a wo/man by the name of..
FULL NAME

She calls her/himself the...
SUPERHERO NAME

S/he says s/he has a unique ability to...

....
SUPER POWER

We talked for about ....minutes about...

....
TOPICS OF CONVERSATION (INDUSTRY, PASSIONS, PROBLEMS, ETC.)

I thought what s/he had to say was..
FEELING ABOUT YOUR INSIGHTS & EXPERTISE

Here's her/his card. I think you should really check out her/his website and................

....
ACTION YOU WANT THEM TO RECOMMEND THEIR FRIEND TAKES

2. PARKING LOT AFFIRMATION

Who do you have to BE when you enter this room to have someone talk about you like that to someone else?

Example: I am the PurposeFinder. When I am present, people
1. see what's possible for their own lives
2. feel more motivated to accomplish their goals
3. hear their inner voice a lot clearer

I am independent AND available.

I am about giving (not getting), passion (not profession), listening (not talking), and being a contribution (not business cards).

I am the..!
                    SUPERHERO NAME

When I am present, people (see/feel/hear/taste/smell/sense/etc.):

1..
        WHAT HAPPENS FOR PEOPLE'S LIVES WHEN YOU ARE AROUND

....

2..
        WHAT HAPPENS FOR PEOPLE'S LIVES WHEN YOU ARE AROUND

....

3..
        WHAT HAPPENS FOR PEOPLE'S LIVES WHEN YOU ARE AROUND

....

3. WHAT WOULD A .... **DO IN THIS SPACE?**
                                  SUPERHERO NAME

What do you have to DO when you enter this room to have someone talk about you like that to someone else?

Example:
1. Ask people who look lost what they're looking for and point them in the right direction
2. Introduce people with similar purposes
3. Ask "So what are you passionate about?" instead of "So, what do you do?"
4. Guide people to resources that will help them on their journey

1. ....
....

2. ....
....

3. ....
....

4. ....
....

5. ....
....

6. ....
....

4. YOUR INVITATION TO GO DEEPER

During the exchange of business cards.

I really enjoyed our conversation.

Now I know that when most people exchange business cards, 90% of the time it means that they will never talk again, but if you're open to it, I would like to invite you to a monthly group I host of some pretty amazing people.

It's called a 30 Day Do It group.

Basically, every 30 days, a group of highly ....
                                                            TWO ADJECTIVES (E.G. MOTIVATED OR INTELLIGENT)

....
            DESCRIPTOR OF GROUP (IE GEEKS, YOUNG PROFESSIONALS, ENTREPRENEURS)

get together and set one goal for the month. It's called your new month resolution.

But when you set that goal, you also create a cost for not achieving it. For instance, I bet everyone that I would pay them $40 each if I don't accomplish my goal this month.

The higher the cost you set, the greater the chance that you'll complete your goal.

You can use it for any type of goal — personal, professional, family, physical, financial.

Our next meeting is on .... in ....
                          DAY & DATE & TIME   CITY/LOCATION

I'll include the details in my follow up email.

Seriously, if there is anything in your life that isn't where you want it be, this is the way to move it. On top of that you'll meet more great people.

What's a goal or project you have in mind that you've been stuck or moving slow on?

3.3 HOW TO SHARPEN YOUR 30 SECOND PITCH DELIVERY

Video Time: 5 minutes
Activity Time: 45 minutes

Required Tools:
- mirror

Language:
None

Directions:
1. Rehearse this conversation in the mirror out loud at least 10 times until it flows freely.

DELIVERY

YOU MATTER **I'M CARING**	**YOU:** Hi, How are you? My name is Jullien Gordon. **THEM:** I'm Michelle Smith. **YOU:** Nice to meet you. Who or what brings you here this evening? **THEM:** I'm a good friend of Pip's. We used to work together at ACME Inc. And you? **YOU:** My friend Bill Rutland invited me. He's over there. Great guy! **THEM:** So what do you do?
I'M INDEPENDENT	**YOU:** Well, I'm a PurposeFinder. **THEM:** A PurposeFinder. What's that?
I'M VALUABLE	**YOU:** I make it possible for people who hate their jobs and are dealing with underemployment, underperformance, and underpay experience what it means to make a living doing what you love. **THEM:** Interesting. I haven't heard of that one before. So you have your own company?
I'M AVAILABLE **I'M PASSIONATE**	**YOU:** Actually, I'm not an entrepreneur. That's how I create value within companies. I'm really passionate about helping people and companies grow and create the life they always dreamed of and I envision a world where everyone is making their highest contribution.
I'M LISTENING	What are you passionate about? **THEM:** ....

I'M A CONTRIBUTION TO YOU	YOU: Interesting! Have you met... You two should really meet. She's over there. I'll make sure to introduce you before the evening is over. OR I really need to put you in contact with my friend................................. He shares your passion for .... and I think you two would have a great time together. Have you read.. It's a must read. I'm surprised you haven't heard about it yet. Have you seen... You have got to see this film.
I'M GIVING	Have you heard of... You should check out their website. Let me write it down (on one of my business cards) for you. I'm also going to give you another one of my cards in case you meet anyone tonight or afterward that you think I should know.

DAY 19

3.4 HOW TO SOUND LIKE AN EXPERT AT ANY NETWORKING EVENT

Video Time: 5 minutes
Activity Time: 15 minutes

Required Tools:
None

Language:
None

Directions:
1. Follow the directions below and complete the worksheets.

Top Article
1. Go to http://news.google.com.
2. In the search box, type in your industry (e.g. banking, non-profit, marketing).
3. Choose an interesting article and click on the link.
4. Read it and then use the template below to formulate an interesting opinion for conversation.
5. Also read the comments. They have interesting thoughts and opinions.

Top Blog
1. Go to http://alltop.com.
2. In the search box, type in your industry (e.g. banking, non-profit, marketing).
3. Click on the result that best matches your search term.
4. Choose one of the most popular stories and click on the link.
5. to
6. Also read the comments. They have interesting thoughts and opinions.

Top Book
1. Go to http://www.amazon.com.
2. Select the "Books" category.
3. In the search box, type in your industry (e.g. banking, non-profit, marketing).
4. Under "New Releases" in the upper left, select "Last 90 Days".
5. Copy the book title.
6. Go to http://www.google.com.
7. Paste the book title and hit search.
8. Find and read an article about the book's release.
9. Use the template below to formulate an interesting opinion for conversation.

Top TED.com Talk
1. Go to http://www.ted.com.
2. In the search box, type in your industry (e.g. banking, non-profit, marketing).
3. Choose one of the videos that interest you most.
4. Watch the 20 minute video and then use the template below to formulate an interesting opinion for conversation.

Top Company or Person
1. Go to http://news.google.com.
2. In the search box, type in a company or person's name you want to research.
3. Choose an interesting article and click on the link.
4. Read it and then use the template below to formulate an interesting opinion for conversation.
5. Also read the comments. They have interesting thoughts and opinions.

TOP ARTICLE OR BLOG

.... had a great article I think you should check out
The Blog, Magazine, or Paper Name

on .... The writer's main argument in the article was
     Passion, Problem, Industry

....

....

I really thought that his/her point about ....

was very interesting because..

....

Based on your experience, what do you think about their argument?

TOP BOOK

Have you read..by..
               Book Title   Author

It's about .... His/Her main premise is
              Passion, Problem, Industry

....

....

....

I really thought that his/her point about ....

was very interesting because..

....

What do you think about their premise?

TOP TED.COM TALK

.... gave a great talk at TED I think you should see
Presenter's Name

on .... His/Her main point during the talk was
      Passion, Problem, Industry

....

....

....

I really thought that his/her point about ....

was very interesting because..

....

What do you think about...?
                                                   TED Talk Topic

TOP COMPANY OR PERSON

Have you heard of..? I hear that they are doing
                   Company Name or Person

some pretty awesome work regarding..
                                                  Passion, Problem, Industry

I recently read that..

....

....

....

How do you think that kind of innovation could affect the marketplace?

3.5 HOW TO FIND GREAT NETWORKING EVENTS

Video Time: 6 minutes
Activity Time: 30 minutes

Required Tools:
- computer with internet
- keywords for your industry

Language:
None

Directions:
1. Research the websites below to find potential networking events in your city.
   NOTE: All events can be considered networking events.
2. Use the sites and techniques to find 3 events that may help your career change.

MEETUP.COM
1. Go to http://www.meetup.com.
2. Type in your INDUSTRY and your CITY and hit search.
3. Click the "Calendar of Meetups" button to see all the upcoming events by date.
4. Click on the EVENT or GROUP NAME to get more details.
5. Sign up for Meetup.com to join group and get updates.

ZVENTS.COM
1. Go to http://www.zvents.com.
2. Type in your city or zip code and hit search.

UPCOMING.YAHOO.COM
1. Go to http://upcoming.yahoo.com.
2. Type in "Networking" in the first box and your city in the second box and hit search.

FACEBOOK
1. Go to http://www.facebook.com.
2. In the search box, type "networking & YOUR CITY" (i.e. networking New York).
3. Instead of hitting "Search" click on "See more results for networking."
4. On the left-hand side, click "Events."

YELP.COM
1. Go to http://www.yelp.com/events.
2. Type in your city and hit search.
3. Right under the search box, hit "Events."

NETPARTY.COM
1. Go to http://www.netparty.com.
2. Select your city.

NETWORKINGEVENTFINDERS.COM
1. Go to http://networkingeventfinders.com/calendars/index.php?calendar=34&v=w.
2. In the "Calendar" section on the left, find your city.

ALUMNI EVENTS
1. Go to your university or high school's alumni page.
2. Click on "Events" and see if anything is coming up near you.

EVENTFUL
1. Go to http://eventful.com/search?q.
2. Type in your city as the keyword.

3. Select the "Events" radio button.
4. Sort by "Date."
5. Limit to "Networking."
6. Also try limiting to "Conferences," "Learning," and "On Campus | Alumni."

EVENTBRITE
1. Go to http://www.eventbrite.com.
2. Type in your City and hit search.
3. In the box on the left, type "Networking" or your industry. Your city should be in the box on the right. Hit search again.
4. Hit sort by "Date" and look through the events until you find something that interests you.

CRAIGSLIST
1. Go to http://www.craigslist.org.
2. Select your city.
3. On the left hand side, click the date on the EVENTS CALENDAR.
4. In the search box, enter "Networking."
5. In the pull down menu, find "All Events" and hit search.
6. Scroll down and look for upcoming dates.

EVENT 1

NAME: ....

DATE:..TIME:..

LOCATION:...FEE:.......................................

EVENT 2

NAME: ....

DATE:..TIME:..

LOCATION:...FEE:.......................................

EVENT 3

NAME: ....

DATE:..TIME:..

LOCATION:...FEE:.......................................

3.6 HOW TO FOLLOW UP USING T.E.C.H.

Video Time: 5 minutes
Activity Time: 0 minutes

Required Tools:
- email account
- cell phone with text messaging
- Twitter account

Language:
None

Directions:
1. After meeting someone new, use these methods to keep the relationship alive.

T.E.C.H.

TEXT or TWEET (Tomorrow morning)

Hi Alex, It's Jullien. Great meeting you at last night's event. Expect an email by Thursday.

EMAIL (24-48 hours after the text message)

SUBJECT: Hi Alex, It's Jullien from Tuesday's Speed Networking Event

BODY: Hi Alex,

Thanks for the good conversation and laughs last night. I'm glad we met.

1. Recommendations

Check out the recommendations we discussed when you get a chance.

Daniel Pink's Drive 2.0: http://www.amazon.com/Drive
The HR Organization: http://www.hrorg.org

2. www.julliengordon.com

My resume 1.0, resume 2.0, Facebook, LinkedIn, Twitter, and other contact information can all be found here. Please forward it on to anyone who you think it will be valuable to.

3. 30 Day Do It group

If you're interested, my next 30 Day Do It group is on June 6, 2010, at 7pm at 1342 Longley Ave, Brooklyn, NY. I hope you can make it. If not this month, then sometime in the near future.

Take care,

CALL (1 week later if no response)

Voicemail: Hi Alex, It's Jullien Gordon. We met briefly at the networking event last Tuesday. I'm just following up to 1. make sure you got my email with the information I promised and 2. see if you had 10-15 minutes to give me some industry insight and career advice. My number is (646) 875-8477. Again that's (646) 875-8477. Thanks in advance.

WHEN TECHNOLOGY FAILS TO SUSTAIN THE RELATIONSHIP....

HOST (one week before your event)

Hi Alex,

I hope all is well. I just want to remind you that the young professional's 30 Day Do It group is happening on June 6, 2010, at 7pm at 1342 Longley Ave, Brooklyn, NY. I hope you can make it. If not this month, then sometime in the near future.

Take care,

OR choose another event that you think that person would gain extreme value from. Make the invitation sound exclusive (i.e. I want to invite you as one of my two guests to a forum of 30 amazing entrepreneurs, techies, and geeks)

ONCE YOU HAVE THEIR ATTENTION, SIMPLY FOLLOW THE GET LINKED IN FORMAT

DAY 20

3.7 HOW TO EXECUTE A POWERFUL 30-MINUTE GET LINKED IN CONVERSATION

Video Time: 5 minutes
Activity Time: 45 minutes

Required Tools:
None

Language:
- cell phone contacts

Directions:
1. Arrange a get linked in call with one of your Target 30 via phone or email.
2. Complete the pre-call worksheet.
3. Walk through the script step-by-step.

30-MINUTE GET LINKED IN FORMAT

1. THANK YOU & WHY YOU CHOSE THEM:..

....

....

2. MY PURPOSE STATEMENT:..

....

....

3. POINT A: WHERE AM I?...

....

....

4. POINT B: WHERE AM I TRYING TO GO?..

....

....

5. TOOLS I HAVE:..

....

....

6. OBSTACLES I FACE:...

....

....

If you're open to it, I have some questions written down that I would like to go through, otherwise you can just take what I've shared so far and give your advice.

1. GET ME RIGHT (ADVICE)
- Given skills and strengths I have, where do you think I can add the most value?
- Do you have any advice on the resume I sent you and my positioning?
- Where do you see the company/industry going in 5 years?
- What's the biggest problem facing this company/industry right now?

2. GET ME ON (INFORMATION)
- Do you know of any listservs, websites, books, or blogs I should be up-to-date on?
- How do you stay so sharp? What are you reading every day?

3. GET ME OUT (NETWORKING)
- Are there any other events on your calendar that you think would be good for me to meet more people like you?
- If not, when great events come to you, can you email them to me?

4. GET ME IN (OPPORTUNITIES)
- Based on my value proposition, do you have opportunities that you think would be a fit for me?
- Do you know of any opportunities that would fit me?

5. GET ME UP (LEADS)
- Do you have three friends, colleagues, or classmates in decision-making positions that you can recommend me to based on my qualifications?
- Do you know of any companies I should be on the look out for?

ADDITIONAL QUESTIONS & GENERAL ADVICE

THANK YOU

3.8 HOW TO NETWORK UP & FIND MENTORS

Video Time: 5 minutes
Activity Time: 30 minutes

Required Tools:
None

Language:
None

Directions:
1. Identify 8 people who are older than you but still working (e.g. parents, professors, teachers, aunts & uncles, friends' parents, community leaders, clergy, your accountant, doctor, etc.).
2. Reach out to each one of them using the email template or call script below and see if they know anyone who can help you.
3. Repeat the process until you get at least four new leads or introductions.

NAME & NAME OF PERSON YOU MAY HAVE TO GO THROUGH	THEIR CONTACT INFORMATION
Mr. Jones **Connection:**	*Dr. Smith* *(243) 543-9854* *drsmith@gmail.com*
Connection:	
Connection:	
Connection:	
Connection:	
Connection:	

NAME & NAME OF PERSON YOU MAY HAVE TO GO THROUGH	THEIR CONTACT & INFO
Mr. Jones **Connection:**	*Dr. Smith* *(243) 543-9854* *drsmith@gmail.com*
Mr. Jones **Connection:**	
Mr. Jones **Connection:**	
Mr. Jones **Connection:**	
Mr. Jones **Connection:**	
Mr. Jones **Connection:**	

EMAIL OR CALL TO OLDER PERSON

Hi Dad,

I hope all is well.

I need your help finding a mentor in the...
                                                                        Industry, Field

I'm ready to accelerate my career, but I want proper guidance and direction, so I'm seeking to gain wisdom from people who are already where I want to be.

Can you think of any
- friends
- friends of friends
- classmates, or
- clients that you can connect me with?

Flip through your cell phone numbers and see who pops up. If not, even ideas of where to look or go will help.

I appreciate your support.

Sincerely,

EMAIL OR CALL TO THEIR CONTACT

SUBJECT: Hi Dr. Smith, Recommended by Bob Jones

BODY: Thanks Mr. Jones,

Hi Dr. Smith,

My name is Jullien Gordon and I've been seeking a mentor with experience in

.... I recently shared what I was looking for
            Industry, Field

with Mr. Jones and you were the first person that came to mind.

I'm ready to accelerate my career, but I want proper guidance and direction, so I'm seeking to gain wisdom from people who are already where I want to be.

I'm currently ....
                                           Point A

but my goal is to ....
                                           Point B

I would love to meet you via phone or in person. Please let me know when you have 10-15 minutes to talk.

Sincerely,

DAY 21

3.9 HOW TO ASK AND ENGAGE MENTORS

Video Time: 9 minutes
Activity Time: 60 minutes

Required Tools:
- Microsoft Word or Google Docs

Language:
Social Capital = Who you know and who knows you

Directions:
1. Take your Target 30 list from the previous module.
2. Customize this email template below for "network up" individual.
3. Use the Mentorship Meeting Guide for your first meeting or call.

EMAIL OR PHONE SCRIPT TO ASK

Dear ....,

THANK YOU

First and foremost, I just want to thank you for your contribution to ....

.... through your amazing work on
        General Industry, Field, Company

....
                        Main area of work

You are one of my pioneers and I'm excited to build a relationship with you.

MY PURPOSE STATEMENT

I admire your journey from.. to now. I'm on a similar journey
                       Where you are (e.g. college)

of my own and after some deep introspection, I've discovered that my purpose is

....

....

THE INVITATION

I know that in order to advance my career and make my greatest contribution to the

.... like you have, I need guidance.
        General Industry, Field, Company

I'm not sure if you had or have mentors or if you already have mentees today, but I would love to explore a mentoring relationship with you. I specifically just need someone to occasionally call on for factual and actionable advice. Please let me know if this is something you would be open to.

Thanks in advance,

Your Name Here

30 MINUTE MENTOR MEETING GUIDE

Date, Time, & Phone	August 1, 2010 at 5pm at 243-534-8756
Why this person?	Rebecca has 15 years of experience in HR
Main Topic/Issue	Career Advancement
Point A: Where am I?	I am currently at a dead end job in marketing and have recently discovered that my purpose is to help organizations keep employees motivated to succeed
Point B: Where am I trying to go?	I am seeking an executive position in human resources at a mid-sized company in the technology sector. I have three target companies.
Questions	- What should I be looking for in a great HR manager? - How do you see marketing being relevant to HR? - What are the companies with the highest retention rates of talent? - Which company do you think would be best for me?

Notes/Advice	- It's not about the size, it's about your leadership and responsibility - Money is secondary to meaning, culture, and team - Ask to do informational interviews - Look on LinkedIn to see if you know anyone there - You may want to position yourself as a recruiter instead of an HR executive given your marketing expertise - You should also consider head hunting firms instead of working for a single corporation
Deliverables	Send Rebecca customized resume and cover letter for each target company one week before next call
Next Meeting Date & Time	September 1, 2010 at 5pm

30 MINUTE MENTOR MEETING GUIDE

Meeting Date & Time	
Mentor's Phone #:	
Main Topic/Issue	
Point A: Where am I?	
Point B: Where am I trying to go?	
Questions	
Notes/Advice	
Deliverables	
Next Meeting Date & Time	

MODULE FOUR

Land Your D.R.E.A.M. Job

DAY 22

4.1 HOW TO LEAVE THE DOOR OPEN AT YOUR OLD JOB

Video Time: 6 minutes
Activity Time: 60 minutes

Required Tools:
- Microsoft PowerPoint

Language:
None

Directions:
1. Submit the following letter four weeks in advance of quitting your current job.
2. Create your off-boarding presentation.

4 WEEKS NOTICE

Dear ....,
         Boss or HR

I am writing this letter to inform you that I will be leaving my current position as

.... as of ....
   Position Name at Company Name   Quit Date

The past .... have been remarkable. During my time
         Time You've Worked There

I was able to create significant value by: (NEW POINT A TO B BULLETS ON RESUME)

* ....

* ....

* ....

* ....

The primary reason I am leaving is the result of deep introspection that has helped me clarify my life purpose. I see opportunities in the marketplace that will allow me to align my passions and profession, while also solving meaningful problems for real people.

I am submitting my notice 2 weeks in advance because I would love to help with the hiring and training of whoever fills my role so that everything transitions smoothly.

Granted your permission, I would also love to host a 15 minute "off-boarding" presentation to say thank you to all of my colleagues as a group before I go.

I am open to talking in greater detail about my decision. Thanks again for this opportunity to be a part of something so great.

Sincerely,

OFF-BOARDING SLIDES

SLIDE 1 TITLE: Cover Page
- Company logo
- Name
- Presentation Title
- Date

SLIDE 2 TITLE: My Top 3-5 Goals (in coming here)
- One ultimate goal
- 3-5 sub-goals

SLIDE 3 TITLE: My Updated Resume
- 10 new point A to B bullet points using the 13Cs

SLIDE 4 TITLE: My High Moments & Low Moments
- 5-8 high moments
- 3-5 low moments

SLIDE 5 TITLE: Special Thank Yous
- Include everyone in some way
- Be specific about what you're thankful for (i.e. Nicole: for your trust & creative freedom)

SLIDE 6 TITLE: My Wish List
- Have fun, but also be serious
- For the CEO
- For your manager
- For your team
- For secretary (i.e. a staple gun to shoot people who steal her staple)
- For the IT guy
- For other people and departments
- For the company as a whole

SLIDE 7 TITLE: My Next Steps
- Your new company
- Your new title
- Your new responsibilities

SLIDE 8 TITLE: My Contact Information
- Name
- Email
- LinkedIn
- Phone (Optional)

DAY 23

4.2 HOW TO USE THE TIME YOU STILL HAVE AT YOUR OLD JOB TO GET YOUR NEW JOB

Video Time: 4 minutes
Activity Time: 60 minutes

Required Tools:
None

Language:
None

Directions:
1. Identify 3 small problems in your organization that you think are solvable.
2. Select the one that you think you can personally have the most impact on with the time you have left.
3. Define how you will know that you've positively impacted the problem.
4. Create an action plan to solve the problem in the allotted time.

BIG BANG PROJECT

1. IDENTIFY THREE PROBLEMS YOU SEE IN YOUR ORGANIZATION RIGHT NOW AND THE METRIC ASSOCIATED WITH THEM

1..

METRIC:..

2..

METRIC:..

3..

METRIC:..

2. CIRCLE THE PROBLEM YOU THINK YOU CAN MAKE THE MOST IMPACT ON IN THE TIME YOU HAVE LEFT. (NOTE: YOU WILL USE THIS IN YOUR INTERVIEW & ON YOUR RESUME)

3. YOU WILL KNOW THAT YOU POSITIVELY IMPACTED THE PROBLEM WHEN...

YOU'VE...

AND THE METRIC MOVES FROM..................................TO................................

4. CREATE AN ACTION PLAN TO SOLVE THE PROBLEM

X	ACTION ITEM	DUE DATE

4.3 HOW TO USE GOOGLE & OTHER JOB SEARCH ENGINES TO SEARCH FOR JOBS FASTER

Video Time: 11 minutes
Activity Time: 15 minutes

Required Tools:
- a Gmail account

Language:
None

Directions:
1. Read the similarities and differences between searching on Google and searching You-goal.
2. Go to http://www.google.com/help/cheatsheet.html to learn more about Google's search operators.

SIMILARITIES & DIFFERENCES BETWEEN GOOGLE & YOU-GOAL

SIMILARITIES	DIFFERENCES
You have to write/type to clarify what you're looking for	Google yields millions of results in seconds You-goal will yield a few unique results over a lifetime
After searching, you still have to dig through the search results	Google doesn't know anything about you as a seeker You-goal is the expert on your life and indexes your experiences
Though search is a discovery process, you'll know it when you've found what you're looking for	Google's (Page Rank) algorithm is private You-goal's journey is partially private and partially public
The results will only be as good as the thought you put into the keywords and phrases	Google will yield the same results for the same keywords and phrases for everyone You-goal's results will be unique for each seeker

BASIC SEARCH OPERATORS

OPERATOR EXAMPLE	FINDS PAGES CONTAINING...
consulting jobs	the words consulting and jobs
consulting OR consultant	either the word consulting or the word consultant
"is now hiring"	the exact phrase "is now hiring"
jobs −recession	the word jobs but NOT the word recession
+career	only the word career, and not the plural or any tenses or synonyms

OPERATOR EXAMPLE	FINDS PAGES CONTAINING...
~teaching jobs	jobs info for both the word teaching and its synonyms: professor, instructor, etc
define:computer	definitions of the word computer from around the Web
red * blue	the words red and blue separated by one or more words
I'm Feeling Lucky	takes you directly to first web page returned for your query
facilitate site:www.idealist.org	the words "facilitate" ONLY within www.idealist.org
related:www.mckinsey.com	similar content as www.mckinsey.com (which is essentially their competitors/counterparts)

USING GOOGLE TO FIND LOCAL JOBS
1. Go to http://www.google.com.
2. Type in "[JOB/FUNCTION]" and "City" e.g. "mechanical engineer Oakland" (542,000 results).
3. Put quotations around mechanical engineer --> "mechanical engineer" Oakland (207,000 results).
4. Click "advanced search" and click "Date, usage rights, numeric range, and more."
5. Change "Date" to "past week" (49,000 results).
6. Change "Date" to "past 24 hours" (12,000 results).

USING GOOGLE TO FIND NEW JOB OPENINGS
1. Go to http://www.google.com.
2. Type in "[JOB/FUNCTION] jobs" e.g. "consulting jobs" and hit search.
3. On the left, click "More" and then click "Updates."
4. Review the Twitter, Facebook, & FriendFeed for opportunities.

USING GOOGLE TO FIND A NICHE & POSITION YOURSELF
1. Go to http://www.google.com.
2. Type in [JOB/FUNCTION] and hit search.
3. On the left, click "More search tools."
4. Click "Wonder Wheel."
5. Click on the link that says [JOB/FUNCTION] jobs.
6. Continue to do this and observe the other related niche job titles that branch out.

USING GOOGLE TO SEE WHERE YOUR PROFESSION HAS BEEN & WHERE IT'S GOING
1. Go to http://www.google.com.
2. Type in [JOB/FUNCTION] and hit search.
3. On the left, click "More search tools."
4. Click "Timeline."
5. Click the right side of the timeline bar graph after 2000.
6. Click on "2010."
7. Look for trends, company names, interesting news, and opportunities.

EXTRA CREDIT: USING GOOGLE ADWORDS TO ATTRACT ATTENTION
1. Watch this video at http://www.youtube.com/watch?v=7FRwCs99DWg.
2. Identify the four top people in your industry that you want to hire you.
3. Go to https://adwords.google.com.
4. Create an ad for each one of them linking back to your resume webpage.
5. Make sure your bid is extremely low.
6. Take down the ad after they reach out to you.

DAY
24

4.4 HOW TO CREATE YOUR VERY OWN JOB "PERCH" ENGINE

Video Time: 6 minutes
Activity Time: 15 minutes

Required Tools:
- Internet
- a Gmail account

Language:
None

Directions:
1. Choose 6 keywords that may yield job opportunities in your target industry.
2. Setup a daily Google Alert at http://www.google.com/alerts based on your selected keywords.
3. Target your job search and test out the search operators on 400+ other job search engines listed here: http://www.careerchangechallenge.com/400-online-job-search-engines/.

CREATE YOUR DAILY JOB "PERCH" ENGINE

1. Choose 6 search terms that you want Google to inform you about daily
EXAMPLES: "Consulting jobs," "McKinsey"

1. .... 4. ....

2. .... 5. ....

3. .... 6. ....

2. Go to http://www.google.com/alerts and enter your search term
EXAMPLES: "Consulting jobs" OR "McKinsey"

TARGET COMPANIES

EXAMPLE: "McKinsey" OR "Deloitte" OR "BCG" OR "Booz"

TARGET POSITIONS

EXAMPLE: "consulting jobs" OR "marketing jobs" OR "sales jobs"

EXAMPLE: "looking for consultants" OR "looking for marketers"

EXAMPLE: "hiring teachers" OR "looking for teachers"

OTHER KEY PHRASES

"job openings" OR "looking for qualified candidates" OR "looking for qualified applicants" OR "send your resume" OR "now hiring" OR "job opportunities" OR "looking to expand" OR "new market" OR "merges with" OR "fastest growing"

USING TWITTER

http://www.hotjobsresources.com/rrc/twitter/?utm_source=HJcareerarticles&utm_medium=careerarticles&utm_campaign=Twitter

4.5 HOW TO USE FACEBOOK, LINKEDIN, & TWITTER TO FIND JOBS

Video Time: 8 minutes
Activity Time: 40 minutes

Required Tools:
- Facebook account
- LinkedIn account

Language:
None

Directions:
1. Follow the directions below to identify job opportunities and find out who you already know that works for the companies that you want to work for.

RESEARCHING COMPANIES & JOBS

LINKEDIN

Find the companies where you know people & how many job openings they have
1. Go to http://www.linkedin.com/companies?trk=tab_compy.
2. Narrow your search by industry, location, country, postal code, company size.

Search your target companies & find the people you are closest to
1. Go to http://www.linkedin.com/companies?trk=hb_tab_compy.
2. Type in one of the names of your target companies.
3. Click "Follow company."
4. Click the same link that now says "Stop following" to edit the "Notification Settings" to get notified when job opportunities are posted.

Now that LInkedIn is working for you, change your notification settings
1. Go to https://www.linkedin.com/secure/settings?msgdelivprefs=&goback=.aas.
2. Change your settings to immediately or weekly based on the urgency of your career change.

FACEBOOK

Find the companies where you know people.
1. Go to http://www.facebook.com/friends/edit/.
2. Click the "Choose an option..." box.
3. Select "Work."
4. Click "Choose an option..." again and see the companies that you know the most people at and how many people you know.
5. Select a company to see who you know there.
6. Go to their profile, grab their email address, and send them a professional email expressing your interest in their company with a link to your website and your resume attached.

Check friends' status updates
1. Go to http://www.facebook.com/search/.
2. In the search box on the left, type "hiring" and hit search.
3. Scroll down to the bottom of the page and click "View All Post By Friends."

TWITTER

Find opportunities without registering for anything
1. Go to http://twitter.com/search?q#search?q=%23jobs OR http://twitter.com/search?q#search?q=%23job.
2. Scan the jobs that are listed.
3. Do multiple searches using each of your keywords from the Google Alerts module.
4. For more advanced searches, go to http://search.twitter.com/advanced.

Find opportunities using http://tweetajob.com
1. Go to http://www.twitter.com and create an account if you don't already have one.
2. Go to http://tweetajob.com/jintro.
3. Login with your Twitter account by clicking the "Sign in with Twitter" button.
4. Click the "Allow" button. You will be redirected back to http://tweetajob.com.
5. Update your profile at http://tweetajob.com/jeditprofile and click "Save."
6. Go to http://tweetajob.com/jeditcategory and select your job categories and click "Save."
7. Click on "My Jobs" (http://tweetajob.com/jprofile) to see all the listings relevant to you.
8. Scroll down to the map on the right and add any other cities you are willing to work in.

For more information on how to use Twitter to search for jobs, download this FREE ebook: http://twitterjobsearchebook.files.wordpress.com/2010/02/tweetajob_updfeb10_ebook.pdf.

DAY 25

4.6 HOW TO PROPERLY RESEARCH A CAREER PATH FOR FIT-NESS

Video Time: 4 minutes
Activity Time: 25 minutes

Required Tools:
None

Language:
Fit-ness = alignment between who you truly are and who an organization or industry needs/wants and will allow you to be

Directions:
1. Shift all of the career path possibilities you came up with from earlier pages to the worksheet below.
2. For each career path, calculate your fit-ness score by marking all of the cylinders that each career aligns with for you.
3. Choose the 5 career paths that align with the most cylinders to begin your research.

TOP 12 CAREER PATHS (in no particular order)	FIT-NESS						
	PRINCIPLES	PASSIONS	PROBLEMS	PEOPLE	POSITIONING	PIONEERS	PICTURE	POSSIBILITY
1								
2								
3								
4								
5								
6								
7								
8								
9								
10								
11								
12								

Fit-ness:
Refer back to your 8 Cylinders of Success from the first section.

Problems It Solves:
Get problem or question by asking people who work(ed) on the career path.

Top 3 Daily Actions:
Get the top three verbs from asking people who work/ed on the career path.

People I Know:
Conduct searches on Facebook and LinkedIn with similar career paths or job titles.

Pioneers:
Do a Google search for "pioneer in [FUNCTION] e.g. "pioneer in consulting." Skip over any results that look like companies. Look for names and pronouns like "he" or "she."

Job Boards:
Refer back to the list of 300+ job boards given or do a Google search for "[INDUSTRY/FUNCTION] jobs" (e.g. "consulting jobs") and look for sites in the first page of results.

Associations:
Do a Google search for "[INDUSTRY/FUNCTION] association" (ie "education association" or "teaching association") and look through the first page of results.

Salary Range:
Go to http://www.payscale.com/index/US/Job, http://www.salary.com or http://www.glassdoor.com.

Current Trends:
Go to http://biz.yahoo.com/ic/ind_index.html and find your industry to see how it's doing financially. Go to http://www.prnewswire.com/search/advanced/ and search industry to see the latest mentions about your industry.

Types/Niches:
Do a Google search for "types of [FUNCTION]" (e.g. "types of engineers").

Applied Industries:
Go to http://www.payscale.com/index/US/Job and find your job title & scroll to industries.

Barriers To Entry & Requirements:
This should be outlined in the job description or posting.

Prospective Companies:
Go to http://www.vault.com/wps/portal/usa/companies and find your industry or function. If it's not there, do a Google search for "best [FUNCTION] companies" or "top [FUNCTION] companies" e.g. "top life coaching companies."

Career Path:..

Fit-ness
[] Principles [] Passions [] Problems [] People [] Positioning [] Pioneers [] Picture [] Possibility

Research

Problems It Solves:..

Top 3 Daily Actions:...

People I Know:...

Pioneers:..

Job Boards:..

Associations:...

Salary Range:..

Current Trends:...

Types/Niches:..

Applied Industries:...

Barriers To Entry & Requirements

Education:.. Years of Experience:..................

Certificates/Licenses:..

Other:..

Prospective Companies

....

....

....

4.7 HOW TO PROPERLY RESEARCH A COMPANY SO YOU INTERVIEW AS FEW TIMES AS POSSIBLE

Video Time: 4 minutes
Activity Time: 40 minutes

Required Tools:
- company website
- job description
- insider information (if possible)

Language:
None

Directions:
1. Use the template below to evaluate the fit-ness of each company you are considering working for.

EXAMPLE

Company: Apple

Job Title: iTunes Store Product Marketing Manager

The Company (from company website & about us page)

	8 CYLINDERS OF SUCCESS	FIT?
Principles	innovation, easy of use, revolutionary	X
Passions	creating cool technology products	X
Problem	how to create tools that help people create what they want	X
People	Cultural Creatives	X
Positioning	world's leading technology & innovation company	X
Pioneers	Microsoft	X
Picture	a world where people are free to create	X
Possibility	a world with no unrealized ideas	X
Purpose	to create technology that helps people turn ideas into reality	X

The Job (from job description & posting)

	8 CYLINDERS OF SUCCESS	FIT?
Principles	ease of use, nice design	X
Passions	working with UI, software engineering, working with media	X
Problem	how to expand the use of iTunes with existing and new customers	X
People	media consumers (music, videos, books, etc)	X
Positioning	the world's leading multi-media distribution center	X
Pioneers	none	X
Picture	a one-stop shop for every form of digital media	X
Possibility	being able to listen, watch, & experience what you want instantly	X
Purpose	to create a shopping experience that helps people find & buy media	X

Company:..

Job Title:..

The Company (from company website & about us page)

	8 CYLINDERS OF SUCCESS	FIT?
Principles		
Passions		
Problem		
People		
Positioning		
Pioneers		
Picture		
Possibility		
Purpose		

The Job (from job description & posting)

	8 CYLINDERS OF SUCCESS	FIT?
Principles		
Passions		
Problem		
People		
Positioning		
Pioneers		
Picture		
Possibility		
Purpose		

The Culture

	PLACES TO RESEARCH	GREAT	GOOD	BAD
Company	Go to http://www.glassdoor.com			
Industry	Go to http://biz.yahoo.com/ic/ind_index.html			
Stocks	Go to http://finance.yahoo.com			
Press	Go to http://www.prnewswire.com/search/advanced/ and search industry & company			
News	Go to http://news.google.com/			
Interviews	Go to http://www.vault.com, type in company & read "Reviews" OR Go to http://www.glassdoor.com, type in company & click "Interviews"			

The Lifestyle

	LIFESTYLE NOTES	GREAT	GOOD	BAD
Work Life Balance				
City & Commute				
Salary & Bonus				
Benefits & Vacation				
Leadership/Mgrs.				
Product/Service				
Teammates				
Growth Opportunity				
Feedback/Mentor				

www.CareerChangeChallenge.com   Copyright © 2010 Jullien Gordon

DAY 26

4.8 HOW TO IDENTIFY THE PROBLEM THEY ARE HIRING YOU TO SOLVE

Video Time: 4 minutes
Activity Time: 20 minutes

Required Tools:
- job description

Language:
Skill = an action by which someone can replicate success more frequently than the average person

Directions:
1. Read the job description, especially the bullet points.
2. Identify 5 problems that position/action is supposed to solve.
3. Write your experience dealing with each problem listed.

Problem:..

My Experience:..

....

....

Problem:..

My Experience:..

....

....

Problem:..

My Experience:..

....

....

Problem:..

My Experience:..

....

....

Problem:..

My Experience:..

....

....

4.9 HOW TO REPURPOSE, REPOSITION, & TRANSFER EVERYTHING YOU'RE DOING NOW TO HELP YOU STAND OUT

Video Time: 4 minutes
Activity Time: 60 minutes

Required Tools:
- job description

Language:
Skill = an action by which someone can replicate success more frequently than the average person

Directions:
1. Print the job description of the job that interests you.
2. Take your "How-Tos" from Module 1.19 in the workbook.
3. Connect your "How-To" to a skill listed in the job description.
4. Identify the skill that you're good at but your new employer may think is irrelevant.
5. Find a news story that connects that skill to your industry or job.
6. Create an analogy or extended metaphor that shows how the thought process behind the "irrelevant skill" and industry or job are similar.

LIST ALL OF THE SKILLS REQUIRED IN THE JOB DESCRIPTION	LIST THE JOB, EVENT, CLIENT, OR STORY YOU HAVE TO TELL ABOUT THIS SKILL
EX.	Route 66 Tour
1	
2	
3	
4	
5	
6	
7	
8	
9	
10	
11	
12	
13	
14	
15	
16	
17	
18	
19	
20	

READ THE JOB DESCRIPTION AND LIST THE SKILLS OR REQUIREMENTS THAT ARE CLOSEST TO WHAT YOU KNOW HOW TO DO

developing and delivering presentations, lead a team of 20 associates

1	
2	
3	
4	
5	
6	
7	
8	
9	
10	
11	
12	
13	
14	
15	
16	
17	
18	
19	
20	

Tell a story about how this industry needs your unique skill by finding a relevant news story:

Example: I did search on cooking & consulting on Google News and got this story http://www.patriotledger.com/news/x1195009410/Retail-chains-find-they-can-grow-with-smaller-outlets

Google News search for .... and ....
　　　　　　　　　　　　　　　　Industry/Job　　　　　　　　　　　　　　　"Irrelevant Skill"

Article Summary:..

....

....

....

....

....

....

....

Create an analogy or extended metaphor about how the two things are linked:

I think of .... the same way I think about ....
　　　　　　　Industry/Job　　　　　　　　　　　　　　　　　　　　　　　　"Irrelevant Skill"

How so?..

....

....

....

....

DAY 27

4.10 HOW TO ANSWER THE TOP 20 INTERVIEW QUESTIONS WITH CONFIDENCE

Video Time: 16 minutes
Activity Time: 60 minutes

Required Tools:
None

Language:
None

Directions:
1. Fill in the blanks for the interview questions below.
2. Create flashcards with the interview questions.
3. Rehearse your answers for the day.

1. So, tell me a little about yourself.
- Give them your **30 second pitch** in a conversational manner.

2. Why are you looking (or why did you leave your last job)?
- As indicated by my **resume**, I created as much value as I felt I possibly could at my last company given the leadership, resources, and responsibilities I had.
- I recently did some very deep self-exploration that helped me discover my purpose and passions and I believe that it's not only possible to align your passions and profession, but that it is also your competitive advantage to do so.
- When someone asks me, "So what do you do?" I want to be able to answer "I'm just me all day" because that means I'm fully present and therefore extremely productive. I believe that is possible here.

3. Tell me what you know about this company.
- Recite their **8 Cylinders of Success** back to them...
- "I know that this company is based on the principles of..."
- "I know that everyone here is passionate about _____, _____, and solving the problem of (or answer the question) _____ for people who [CUSTOMER HERE i.e. middle class families, moms, professionals, etc.]."
- "I know that you're committed to being the world's best at _____ and ultimately you envision a world where _____ and it's possible for [CUSTOMER HERE] to _____."

4. Why do you want to work at X Company?
- I'm a [**SUPERHERO NAME**] and I have a unique ability to [**SUPERPOWER**].
- My strengths also include [**GALLUP STRENGTHSFINDER STRENGHTS HERE**].
- I think that this combination of skills and strengths will allow me to create extreme value for this organization and I want to be somewhere where I can create value, feel valued, and that aligns with my values.

5. What relevant experience do you have?
- Cite the top three examples/stories you have from the **transferable skills activity.**
- EXAMPLE: "Based on the job description, I know that building an error-free data management is key to the business objectives and I've done that a few times. The most recent example is from my last job where I was given [**POINT A**] and had to move it to [**POINT B**]. My team and I were successful in doing so [**STATISTICS/ RESULTS**] in half the expected time and $100,000 under budget.
- SHOW SOMETHING FROM YOUR RESUME 2.0/PORTFOLIO.

6. If your previous co-workers were here, what would they say about you?

- Pull adjectives from your **retirement speech** and results from your **resume** or **off-boarding presentation** and then can say why each is important and give an example.
- They would say that I am innovative, driven, and personable. When I think about my professional legacy, that's how I want to be remembered and I think they would agree.
- Innovation is important to me because [WHY]. You will see the verb created on my resume quite a few times, for example, [EXAMPLE].
- Drive is important to me because [WHY]. I'm always the first person in the office because I like getting a head start and I work best in the morning.
- Being personable is important to me because [WHY]. I never eat alone. I always seek to get to know my teammates better at work and after work.

7. Have you done anything to further your experience?
- Mention the study of pioneers and your current mentors.
- Mention books and blogs you read as well as your Google Alerts.
- Mention classes, conferences, and certificates.

8. Where else have you applied?
- BEST ANSWER: I've only applied here because I'm certain of the alignment. My metrics for success with my interview strategy was NOT the number of interviews I could get. Instead I focused on researching and finding the right opportunity and dedicated all of my time to getting here. (I think people just interview like crazy when they don't know what they want. If it doesn't work out, I will seek the next best alignment.).
- If you have applied to more than one place, tell them up to three.

9. How are you when you're working under pressure?
- It's funny you should ask that because I put myself under pressure every month.
- I think that we really get to know who we are under pressure.
- So I lead a monthly goal setting group for people with personal and professional goals called the 30 Day Do It. When you set a goal, you also have to create a cost for not achieving your goal. Now that's pressure!
- Through leading this group, I've come to learn that I am [ANSWER HERE] under pressure. But because I intentionally put myself in pressure situations, there isn't much variance between who I am under pressure or without it.

10. What motivates you to do a good job?
- I have this equation I use to motivate myself: Problems + Passion = Purpose. When I can find a meaningful and challenging problem that affects people's lives and then use my passions to solve it, that's when I'm most purpose-filled and motivated.

- For me, purpose is the highest form of motivation because it's intrinsic and when I'm motivated from within, that's when I do my best. I think great leaders can pull that out of an individual or team. As for extrinsic motivators, I think they simply support what's within.

11. What's your greatest strength?
- Pull from the Gallup StrengthsFinder 2.0 module. Choose your strength with the most powerful example and tell the Point A to B story.
- My greatest strength is [STRENGTH HERE]. The most vivid example I have is when [Point A]. My ability to [STRENGTH AS VERB] made it possible for [Point B].
- SHOW SOMETHING FROM YOUR RESUME 2.0/PORTFOLIO.

12. What's your biggest weakness?
- Pull from extended metaphor and transferable skills exercise.
- At this moment, I lack some skills and experience, though I think they can be learned quickly.
- For the last few years, I've been developing my [SEEMINGLY IRRELEVANT SKILL], but I recently read an article about how...
- OR For the last few years, I been developing my [SEEMINGLY IRRELEVANT SKILL], but I think of [NEW SKILL] in a similar way. [EXTENDED METAPHOR].

13. Let's talk about salary. What are you looking for?
- Pull this number from your job research on http://www.glassdoor.com or http://www.salary.com and the professional velocity number you came up with in the beginning.
- Practice saying this number with confidence over and over before the interview
- I value my work at $50/hour and when you multiply that by a 2,000 hour work year, that's $100,000.
- At the end of the day, I only want to be paid according to the value I create and the size of the problems I solve.

14. Are you good at working in a team?
- Yes. I've worked on teams as large as [##] and as small as [##], but the best team I ever worked on was a team of [##]. [Point A] to [Point B].

15. Tell me a suggestion you have made that was implemented.
- You can tell a Point A to B story for you Big Bang Project at your last job.
- You can also tell the story of the off-boarding process.
- EXAMPLE: You know how employees always get on-boarded, but they never get off-boarded. You look up one day and someone is just gone. Well at my last job, I introduced the idea of off-boarding. Basically, anyone leaving has to give a 15-

minute presentation about the value they created during the time they were there. Now imagine the motivation of an employee during their time here knowing that at some point they are going to have to account for everything they've done. It increases drastically. On top of that, people don't leave with sour tastes in their mouths.
- SHOW SOMETHING FROM YOUR RESUME 2.0/PORTFOLIO.

16. Has anything ever irritated you about people you've worked with?
- The only thing that irritates me are people who complain without commitment to change. If I see something is wrong for the company, our customers, or my own colleagues I'm willing to propose a new idea that may change it and increase everyone's satisfaction.

17. Would you rather work for money or job satisfaction?
- I believe you can have both. I don't think you have to choose between one or the other.
- Just about every person who has created extreme value in the world loved what they were doing.
- I think people who make this tradeoff end up unemployed, underemployed, or burned out which is of no value to anyone.
- EXTRA: In the book "Success Built To Last," Jerry Porras studied 200 of the world's most successful people including former presidents, gold medalist, CEOs, and more and the number one thing he found was they they all followed their passions. Granted they all aren't making the same income, but their life satisfaction is probably equal.

18. Are you willing to put the interests of X Company ahead of your own?
- The reason I am interviewing here is because I believe that my personal interests and the company's interests are extremely aligned, therefore, I won't have to put one in front of the other because they are one in the same.

19. So, explain why I should hire you.
- I am super focused on creating value. Period.
- My commitment to this company is to create more value than I take in the form of salary and benefits using the assets and resources you give me. My professional legacy shows that wherever I go, for however long I'm there, I make an impact.
- If after 3 months, I haven't demonstrated that I can successfully do that and other people can, then I shouldn't be here.
- My resume is an indicator of the quality of work I will resume (pronounced re-zoom) here if given the opportunity.

20. Finally, do you have any questions to ask me?

Company Culture
- What has been your most rewarding/significant project or experience working here?

Position
- Sometimes job descriptions don't tell all, so in your own words, how would you define the problem that this position was created to solve?
- And how will my success be measured?
- Why did the last person transition?

Process
- Assuming I advance in the interview process, what would be the next steps?
- When should I expect to hear back from you?

4.11 HOW TO KEEP A POTENTIAL EMPLOYER ENGAGED AFTER THE INTERVIEW

Video Time: 6 minutes
Activity Time: 20 minutes

Required Tools:
- Thank you cards

Language:
None

Directions:
1. Capture what you remember about each interviewer.
2. Send thank you emails.
3. Send thank you cards.
4. Conduct an over-view of your inter-view.

Interview Name:..

Position:.. Email:...

Their response to your significant/rewarding project or experience question:

....

One interesting thing you remember about them (e.g. I ride bike to work everyday.)

....

[] Thank you email sent [] Thank you card mailed

Interview Name:..

Position:.. Email:...

Their response to your significant/rewarding project or experience question:

....

One interesting thing you remember about them (e.g. I ride bike to work everyday.)

....

[] Thank you email sent [] Thank you card mailed

Interview Name:..

Position:.. Email:...

Their response to your significant/rewarding project or experience question:

....

One interesting thing you remember about them (e.g. I ride bike to work everyday.)

....

[] Thank you email sent [] Thank you card mailed

Thank You Email template

Dear..,
      Interviewer's Name

I just want to say thank you for the opportunity to interview with you yesterday.

I appreciate your time, your insights on the organizational culture, and your daily contribution to the company's mission.

I'm excited about the possibility of working with you and bringing the value I have to offer to... as the new ....
              Company Name   Position

After my visit, I'm convinced that there is a fit. Your experience working with/on

....
              Significant project mentioned in interview

characterizes the types of experiences I want to have in my professional career.

I look forward to hearing from the hiring committee within the next week. Until then, I invite you to visit my professional website and blog at www.YOURNAME.com to see my extended resume and a recent article I wrote related to the future of our industry.

Sincerely,
Your Name

Thank You Card template

Dear..,
       Interviewer's Name

I know that I already expressed my gratitude via email, but sometimes efficiency doesn't equal effectiveness, especially when it comes to communication within organizations. Sometimes you have to go the extra mile.

I'm grateful to have advanced to this stage of the interview process and I am glad to have heard your unique perspective on your experience here. I definitely believe that this is a place where I can create value, I will be valued, and I can express my values.

Thanks again!

Sincerely,
Your Name

Over-View Worksheet

Company:……………………………….Position:………………………………………………

What did I learn about myself? (Not for me, I build good rapport, a little nervous, etc.)

………………………………………………………………………………………………………

………………………………………………………………………………………………………

………………………………………………………………………………………………………

What did I learn about the position? (qualities I seek, problem it solves, metrics, etc.)

………………………………………………………………………………………………………

………………………………………………………………………………………………………

………………………………………………………………………………………………………

What did I learn about the company? (nobody was smiling, very quiet, etc.)

………………………………………………………………………………………………………

………………………………………………………………………………………………………

………………………………………………………………………………………………………

What areas do I need to do more research or study in before future interviews?

………………………………………………………………………………………………………

What question/s stumped me?………………………………………………………………….

………………………………………………………………………………………………………

When should I expect to hear back?…………………………………………………………...

If necessary, how can I prepare better for my next interview?………………………………

………………………………………………………………………………………………………

DAY 28

4.12 HOW TO DETERMINE YOUR VALUE & WHAT YOU'RE WORTH

Video Time: 6 minutes
Activity Time: 20 minutes

Required Tools:
None

Language:
None

Directions:
1. Research the following website to determine the high and low range for your position.

Payscale.com
1. Go to http://www.paysclae.com.
2. Select "Job Seeker".
3. Type in your "Expected job title".
4. Type in your "Year in field/career".
5. Select your "Country".
6. Type in your "City".
7. Select your "State and hit "Next".
8. Enter "# of people supervising/managing".
9. Enter any certifications and hit "Next".
10. Select the "Type of employer".
11. Type in your "Product" & hit "Next".
12. Type in the "School you attended," your "Degree," your "Major," and your "Year of Graduation" and hit "Next".
13. Select your "Degree Type" and hit "Next".
14. Click "No thanks, just show me my salary".
15. Write the 25th and 75th percentiles below.
16. (OPTIONAL) Click on the "Company Charts" button on the left to see how different employers value the position.
17. (OPTIONAL) Click on the "Education" button the left to see which degrees yield the highest salaries.
18. (OPTIONAL) Click "GigZig" to see the future career path for your position.

25th Percentile:...75th
Percentile:...

Glassdoor.com
1. Go to http://www.glassdoor.com/Salaries/index.htm.
2. Type in your JOB/FUNCTION and City and then hit "Search".
3. Hit "Advanced Search" to also search by "Industry" and/or "Company".
4. Skim the results to get a feel for the salary range.

Determine Your Range

$____K $_____K

....
COST OF   IDEAL
LIVING   INCOME

1. Add your MONTHLY COST OF LIVING times 12 to the left side of the line above.
2. Add your IDEAL INCOME from earlier to the right side the line above.
3. Mark the low and high range for the position from Payscale.com.
4. Mark the average salary from Glassdoor.com.
5. Based on the five data points above, determine what you're going to ask for.

My asking salary excluding benefits is $..

DAY 29

4.13 HOW TO CREATE A POWERFUL 3 YEAR PLAN & PREPARE FOR YOUR NEXT CAREER MOVE NOW

Video Time: 6 minutes
Activity Time: 60 minutes

Required Tools:
None

Language:
None

Directions:
1. Define three ways that you can develop your personal, intellectual, social, and financial capital in your new position.
2. Write your off-boarding speech from the perspective of 10 years from today.
3. Generate at least one resume bullet point for each of the 13Cs based on what you want your resume to look like after 10 years.

BRIDGE JOB & 4 CAPITALS

Imagine that this is just a bridge job you are planning to maximize and transition from in 18 months or less. Answer the questions below with this mindset.

Personal Capital
What are three ways I can use this position to develop my personal capital?
(e.g. take on uncomfortable/challenging projects, ask for feedback, strengths testing)

1..

2..

3..

4..

5..

Intellectual Capital
What are three ways I can use this position to develop my intellectual capital?
(e.g. paid training, conferences, 3 skills I want to develop, foreign language)

1..

2..

3..

4..

5..

Social Capital

What are three ways I can use this position to develop my social capital?
(i.e. mentors, board of directors, networking events, etc)

1. ....

2. ....

3. ....

4. ....

5. ....

Financial Capital

What are three ways I can use this position to develop my financial capital?
(e.g. future customers for my business, side hustles using my skills, public speaking)

1. ....

2. ....

3. ....

4. ....

5. ....

OFF-BOARDING SPEECH

Directions:

Write your retirement speech as if you were going to work at this company for 10 years. Be sure to include:
- awesome projects and products that you worked on
- real or fictitious people who you helped or who helped you along the way
- your super hero name, and
- results, results, results that impacted the company, customers, or colleagues

...... years and .... months from today, ..., ..., 20.....

NEW RESUME BULLETS

Write one powerful resume bullet point for each of the 13Cs.

1. Customer or Consumer: Write 1-2 bullet points about how you moved a metric related to customers from Point A to B (e.g. loyalty, satisfaction, dollars per purchase, net promoter score, etc.)

....

....

....

2. Cash Flow: Write 1-2 bullet points about how you moved a metric related to cash flow from Point A to B (e.g. increased inflow, decreased outflow, etc.)

....

....

....

3. Company: Write 1-2 bullet points about how you moved a metric related to the company from Point A to B (e.g. rankings in best places to work, # of new clients, labor standards, decrease % of defective products & returns, etc.)

....

....

4. Colleagues: Write 1-2 bullet points about how you moved a metric related to your colleagues from Point A to B (e.g. retention, on-boarding time decrease, grew full-time-equivalents (FTE), # of mentorship relationships established, # of 360-degree feedback sessions completed, % participated in company retreat, increase in job security, etc.)

....

....

5. Community: Write 1-2 bullet points about how you moved a metric related to the community from Point A to B (e.g. # of hours volunteered, matching funds, mentorships, dollars of pro bono work, etc.)

....

....

6. Capital: Write 1-2 bullet points about how you moved a metric related to the capital from Point A to B (e.g. increase in assets, decrease in debt, mergers, acquisitions, division sold, financing raised, etc.)

....

....

7. Culture: Write 1-2 bullet points about how you moved a metric related to the company culture from Point A to B (e.g. employee satisfaction, # of innovative projects, employee safety rating, etc.)

....

....

8. Campaign: Write 1-2 bullet points about how you moved a metric related to an internal or external campaign from Point A to B (e.g. page views, conversion rate, media impressions, subscribers, etc.)

....

....

9. Champion of Change: Write 1-2 bullet points about how you moved a metric related to a change you led from Point A to B (e.g. carbon emissions decrease, switched software & executed national training, shifted market from computers to consulting, etc.)

....

....

10. Communication: Write 1-2 bullet points about how you moved a metric related to the company communication from Point A to B (e.g. integrated a CMS, established meeting process & protocol, created a Wiki to share intelligence, etc.)

....

....

11. Competition: Write 1-2 bullet points about how you moved a metric related to the competition from Point A to B (e.g. passed Toyota for #1 spot, increased market share by 10%, competition closed 5 stores in new market, etc.)

....

....

12. Collaboration: Write 1-2 bullet points about how you moved a metric related to collaboration or partnerships from Point A to B (e.g. built new supplier relationship, landed $100K sponsorship, led cross-divisional team to create new product, etc.)

....

....

13. Concepts: Write 1-2 bullet points about how you moved a metric related to concepts you created from Point A to B (e.g. created a new business line that grew to $4M, revamped lead generation process using my 4Ps framework, etc.)

....

....

DAY 30

4.14 HOW TO HAVE AN AMAZING FIRST 3 MONTHS

Video Time: 7 minutes
Activity Time: 60 minutes

Required Tools:
None

Language:
None

Directions:
1. Meeting #1: Interview your boss about how they define and measure success.
2. Meeting #2: Share your dashboard, retirement speech, and new resume bullet points.
3. Meeting #3: Create another three month "Big Bang Project" and share it with your boss. Ask for approval to allocate time to this important problem. Note that this project may become your new job if you solve a meaningful problem for the company, colleagues, or customers.

MEETING #1: INTERVIEW YOUR BOSS

Our Company's Purpose

In your own words, why does our company exist?

....

....

What is your vision for this company or more specifically our division?

....

....

How is your company or division's success measured? What are the metrics?

....

Your Position's Purpose

In your eyes, what is the purpose of your position?

....

....

What should I come/look to you for?

....

....

My Position's Purpose

In your eyes, what is the purpose of my position?

....

....

How will my success be measured by you? What are the metrics I should be aware of?

....

....

My On-Boarding Process

Do you have any strategic documents that you can share with me so I can learn more about where we are and where we're trying to go?

How is each team member/division on the organization chart critical to our success?

Are there any readings that shaped your view of our company, customer, or positions?

Do you mind if we have 30-minute one-on-one check-in meetings every 30 days?

MEETING #2: DASHBOARD, OFF-BOARDING SPEECH, & RESUME

Dashboard

1. Based on the metrics of success given during the last meeting and what you've observed with the company culture, create a dashboard for yourself
2. Share the dashboard with your manager and ask them if they agree with the metrics you've chosen and how you're measuring them

Off-Boarding Speech

1. Share the speech with your boss so that they can have a clear vision of your vision

Resume

1. Share that with your boss as well

Request ideas and feedback on how to make your vision a reality.

MEETING #3: BIG BANG PROJECT

1. Identify 3 problems you see in your organization right now and the metrics associated with them:

Problem 1...

Metrics:..

Problem 2...

Metrics:..

Problem 3...

Metrics:..

2. Circle the problem you think you can make the most impact on in a short amount of time.

3. You will know that you positively impacted the problem when...

....

and the metric moves from ....to..

4. CREATE AN ACTION PLAN TO SOLVE THE PROBLEM

	ACTION ITEM	DUE DATE

Made in the USA
Charleston, SC
01 April 2011